CW00349186

SUBMITTING TO GOD

Communities of Faith

Submitting to God

Introducing Islam

Vivienne Stacey

Vivienne Stacey

Hodder & Stoughton

LONDON SYDNEY AUCKLAND

British Library Cataloguing in Publication Data
A record for this book is available from the British Library

ISBN 0 340 65646 8

Typeset by Avon Dataset Ltd, Bidford-on-Avon, Warks

Printed and bound in Great Britain by
Clays Ltd, St Ives plc

Hodder and Stoughton
A division of Hodder Headline PLC
338 Euston Road
London NW1 3BH

Contents

Series Editor's Preface   vii
Acknowledgments   ix

  1   Basic World-View   1
  2   Key Figures   8
  3   The Community of the Faithful   26
  4   Sacred Texts   38
  5   Fundamental Doctrines   49
  6   Spirituality and Worship   56
  7   Ethics and Morality   69
  8   Religious Structures   82
  9   Propagating the Faith   92
10   Concluding Reflections   102

Selected Bibliography   105
Glossary of Some Key Arabic Words   108
Index   111

Series Editor's Preface

There is a human tendency to try to present one's own beliefs, values and practices in a good light by deliberately presenting other beliefs, etc. in as bad light as possible. In this series of books, the authors will not be guilty of misrepresentation, but will be guided by a basic Christian principle – that we should love our neighbours as we love ourselves. Therefore, the same respect and generosity will be given to each faith as Christians would wish for their own faith.

In this series on world faiths we are aiming to produce reference works which will be scholarly in terms of their accuracy and authority, completely fair to others, so that members of different faith communities will recognise themselves in the presentations, and also easily accessible to the general reader.

At the same time, they are written from a confident Christian perspective, and in each book the author will engage in a serious dialogue with the beliefs, values and practices of the faith which he/she is presenting. The authors all have genuine knowledge of the faith about which they are writing, personal experience of the community which holds that faith, a proven ability to reflect deeply on the issues involved, and the gift of being a good communicator. They are all practising Christians who are involved in dialogue with people of other faiths and cultures. Their interaction is sensitive and informed.

In each volume we shall explore a distinct faith and meet the community which lives by it. While the aim is to produce resources which capture the essential and timeless beliefs and values of each faith, full attention is given to the major contemporary issues and personalities. In the same way, while it is important to be aware of the global context of each faith, significant attention will be paid to the situation in the United Kingdom.

In order to make it easier to cross-reference among the books in this series, we have organised each book along the same lines. Topics dealt with in the numbered chapters will be the same in each book, no matter what the titles may be. You are therefore invited to join us in a great exploration of the world's faiths.

This particular volume examines Islam, one of the world's major faiths. Islam is followed by vast numbers of people, and is the dominant faith in many countries. It is spreading at a rapid rate in different parts of the world, including Europe. Many people are attracted by the radically simple creed and high moral standards of its sacred writings, whereas others are frightened by what they see as intolerance and a desire for power. What is a properly sensitive and informed response to Islam by non-Muslims? Vivienne Stacey leads us expertly into the Islamic world in this perceptive and focused book.

Walter Riggans

Acknowledgments

No one can look at two or more faiths from the inside at once. My background was secular humanism. Since becoming a Christian in my student days I began to meet people of other faiths. It has been my privilege to spend thirty-six years in Pakistan and to travel widely in the Middle East, North Africa, the Indian subcontinent and Central Asia as well as in Europe and North America. I am particularly indebted to my Muslim friends for sharing insights into their faith. I am also enriched in seeing facets of my own beliefs which I might have missed had I not long pondered on what I observed in Islam.

One of my main concerns in writing this book is particularly to promote understanding between Muslims, humanists, post-modernists, Christians, those of other faiths and those of no faith, who together form the population in the UK. In my own spiritual pilgrimage as a convinced Christian I am still learning from those of other faiths and of no faith.

I wish to express my thanks to my friend and colleague, Miss P. R. Tring, and to my editor, Dr W. Riggans, who have made many helpful suggestions about my manuscript.

Finally, for the sake of the general reader, I have used AD dates throughout the book instead of the Islamic calendar. I also have anglicised some Arabic words, omitting unfamiliar letters and signs.

Vivienne Stacey
Cyprus 1996

Basic World-View

One might well ask why the religion is called Islam and the followers are called Muslims. Those who do not speak Arabic cannot immediately grasp the connection between Islam (the name of the religion) and Muslim (the adherent of the religion). A close look at these two Arabic words *Islam* and *Muslim* shows that both have three letters in common – 's', 'l' and 'm'. They are called radical or root letters. In the word Muslim it is the second 'm' which is the radical letter. Islam means 'submission to God'. The prefix 'm' in Arabic indicates a 'doer' so Muslim means 'one who submits to God'.

ISLAM   =   SUBMISSION to GOD

MUSLIM   =   ONE WHO SUBMITS to GOD

Muslims do not generally like to be called Muhammadans as they do not worship the Prophet Muhammad. Historically Islam started when Muhammad established the city-state of Medina as the centre for the new community of faith in 622. For the rest of the world this marked the beginning of the new religion of Islam with Muhammad as its founder. However, the Muslim view is that Islam is the ideal religion of humankind. The first man, Adam, 'submitted' to God and so was in fact the first Muslim. From then on God has sent prophets to recall humanity to the original ideal faith. Muhammad was the last in a succession of reformers and prophets. The Quran, the Holy Book of Islam, therefore called him 'the seal of the prophets'. So Muhammad is venerated but not worshipped.

We are becoming more and more aware of Muslims. Every fifth person in the world is a Muslim. Through trade and travel, through immigration and natural population growth, over a million Muslims have become part of the multifaith, multicultural society of modern Britain. If you go to your local store for an extra pint of milk you may be served by a Muslim. Your neighbours might be Muslims from Pakistan or Bangladesh. When my nephew was born in a Brighton hospital two doctors from the Indian subcontinent assisted, one of whom was a Muslim. The Muslims in Britain can be divided into the following groups:

1. Students e.g. Malaysians, Egyptians and Nigerians
2. Refugees e.g. Afghans and Iranians
3. Immigrants and settlers e.g. Pakistanis and Bangladeshis
4. British-born second and third generation citizens
5. Tourists e.g. Arabs from Saudi Arabia, Kuwait and Jordan
6. British converts to Islam

The third group – immigrants and settlers, consisting mainly of those who for economic reasons took jobs in the UK – is the largest group.

To be a minority in a geographically small country with a total population of about fifty-six million requires much adjustment and understanding by that minority and by other minorities and, of course, by the majority community. We all need to have a fresh understanding of each other's cultures, customs and beliefs. Behind culture, custom and belief lies world-view. We may not even be aware of world-view. We grow up assuming it. We judge others by our assumptions. The prevailing world-view in Britain is secular humanism. Those who accept the description Christian are often deeply influenced by this non-Christian world-view. The Muslim who grows up in Britain or comes to work or study has a very different world-view affecting his culture, customs and religious beliefs. So to understand ourselves and Muslims and the religion of Islam we must first look at world-view and then at culture, customs and beliefs.

What is World-View?

We need to be aware of our own world-view as we examine
that of others. In this chapter we particularly look at the
Muslim world-view. Being part of a multicultural, multifaith
situation can be very enriching and challenging. I have
experienced this from being in a minority community situation.
I lived for thirty-six years in a country in which the 95 per
cent majority was Muslim. Christians were less than 3 per
cent of the total population. On returning to my native country
of Britain I found that the prevailing worldview was neither
Christian nor Muslim but secular humanist. My Christian
faith has been deepened and my appreciation of other faiths
and cultures has increased as I have sought to understand my
Muslim neighbours and my secular humanist colleagues.
World-view was one of the keys to understanding both myself
and others.

Briefly, world-view is a study of how a people perceive
reality. David Burnett in his fascinating book entitled *Clash
of Cultures* describes it in this way: 'A worldview consists of
the shared framework of ideas held by a particular society
concerning how they perceive the world. Everyday experiences
are fitted into this framework in order to give a totality of
meaning and comprehension to the individual' (p. 13). In
world-view there is a deeper level of assumption than in
philosophy or theology and it is nearly always subconsciously
assumed. Whoever you are you have a world-view. You may
not know that you have one but you live your life with some
basic assumptions which are as natural to you as the air you
breathe. We all tend to look at other world-views from the
perspective of our world-view. At the same time we may be
quite unaware of what our own world-view is, let alone what
the Muslim world-view is.

In his book Dr Burnett has sought to look at several world-
views, studying the following six themes in each: the cosmos,
the self, knowing, community, time and value. In the secular
world-view reason is the basis for establishing the truth about
reality. Human beings are the centre of the universe and
through their minds they can study the material universe. There

is therefore a focus on the natural order which leaves no place for revelation. The universe is controlled by its own laws. Everything must have a logical and scientific explanation. Humanity (the self) is part of this scheme of things. The human mind can examine and document the natural world, often subduing and controlling it. Everything ultimately must have a scientific explanation. Secular humanism sees people as equals not because they are created in the image of God (as in the Christian world-view) but as individuals each having a rational mind.

Community or society is thus an association of individuals, each of whom has the right to develop to their full potential. There is a linear view of time as having an indefinite past, a present and an indefinite future. As the universe is a closed system, ethics are relative and not absolute. At this point the reader may like to consider whether he or she has a secular or some other world-view. For the purpose of this book we should now look at the Muslim world-view.

The Muslim World-View

The Pakistani theologian Maulana Kausar Niazi gave many lectures about the everlasting truths of Islam in the context of the modern world. He summed up the essence of the faith in his book entitled *Fundamental Truths*. Everything is grouped around three words: unity, prophethood and the hereafter. The most important of these three words is unity. Unity is the key to the Muslim world-view. God is One. The opening verse of the first surah of the Quran declares that Allah is 'Lord of the Worlds'. Not only is there a unity of this world and the next but there will be a unity in this world. At the moment this world is divided into two sections, *dar al-islam*, that is, the house of submission or peace where Islam rules and *dar al-harb*, that is, the house of war or that part which is yet to become the house of submission or peace. The ideal is that every state should be ruled by a Muslim and the state governed by Shariah or Islamic law.

In the modern world the Kingdom of Saudi Arabia, with

the creed of Islam ('There is no god but God and Muhammad is his Messenger') on its flag and with the Quran as its constitution, is the nearest to this ideal. With its vision of all the world eventually becoming Muslim it is not surprising to find that Islam is a missionary faith.

There may be many races and ethnic groups but for the Muslim there is one community or *ummah*. A Muslim tradition says that at the end of this world the Prophet Isa (Jesus) will return and make all human beings Muslim. Then there will be only one community. Because of God's unity there is not only one community but also one system. For the community there is one language, Arabic, the language of heaven, in which the Glorious Quran was revealed. The six articles of faith and the five pillars on which they rest are the same throughout the Muslim world. For example, Ramadan, the month of fasting, is marked through all Muslim communities. Even those who do not fast join in the celebration of the daily breaking of the fast and in the feast which marks the end of the month of fasting. Religion is not separated from culture.

In art and architecture it is easy to identify what comes from Muslim culture. Calligraphy is a central feature of Muslim art wherever it is found. The basic structure of the mosque is similar in every place. There are many varieties but in every mosque the direction for prayer is towards Mecca, and the pulpit is visible. Generally there is a clock and a list of prayer times. The minaret is part of the structure as is the large space for prayer. In the mosque there will no pictures of people as these are forbidden. However, there will normally be some beautiful religious inscriptions in Arabic possibly with floral decorations around the borders. The creed of Islam and the Bismillah are those most commonly found. The Bismillah is a much-used phrase which, in full, means 'in the name of Allah, the merciful Lord of mercy'.

Through many centuries the political and religious unity of Islam was demonstrated in the Caliphate which ended in 1924. Since then many Muslims have sought a focus of unity in the Shariah. Another focus of unity has always been the Prophet Muhammad himself. The increase in devotion to and veneration of Muhammad in many areas of the world has partly arisen from the desire for a clear focus for unity. In London practically all the many differing Muslim societies, organisations, sects and groupings are represented when Muhammad's birthday is celebrated publicly. Honouring the Prophet draws together the community of Islam and is an expression of the unity of the community. Muhammad Iqbal (1876–1938), the poet philosopher of the Indian subcontinent, wrote in his long philosophical Persian poem called *Asrar-i-Khudi* or *The Mysteries of Selflessness*:

> Love for the Prophet runs like blood in the veins of the
> community.

In another poem he wrote:

> We are like one rose with many petals, yet one fragrance.
> His is the spirit of the community, and he is one.

The unity of God is for the Muslim a reality which transcends the universe, that operates in both the seen and unseen spheres, that allows no division between sacred and secular or between religious and political. The one God operates through prophets to recall humanity and the world back to the one ideal religion of humankind. Muhammad Iqbal declares in another part of his philosophical poem that since Muslim community is founded upon belief in one God and apostleship it is not bounded by space:

> Our essence is not bound to any place
> The vigour of our wine is not contained
> In any bowl. (p. 29)

We will further explore these themes later in this book. Even such a brief description may make us aware that such a world-view is far removed from that of the secular humanist who sees humanity as the centre of all things and has no strong conviction about the hereafter. The average Western Christian, although taught a world-view by Scripture, has partially forsaken it and privatised religion, dividing sacred from secular, religion from politics and making belief a private affair. Secular humanism exercises that same pressure on Islam in the West but Muslims are doing their best to resist its influence as they are aware of their minority situation. Christians are more laid back. In some ways Muslims and Christians find it hard to understand each other and yet they both find themselves in danger of being entangled by secularism, modernity and post-modernity.

2

Key Figures

Muhammad, the Apostle of Islam

'Muhammad is his Messenger': so runs the second part of
the Muslim creed. Historically Islam started not with the birth
of Muhammad around 570, nor when he first received God's
revelations of parts of the Quran and started his public ministry
in 610. The historical moment was twelve years later in 622.
After persecutions in Mecca, puzzled at his lack of acceptance
as the Prophet of God he left the city with a few followers,
joining other believers in the twin city of Medina and
establishing a city-state. This was the Hijrah or Hegira, which
has been variously translated as Exodus, Flight or Emigration
from Mecca to Medina. The Muslim calendar dates from that
event. Islam was established for all to see. Quickly it became
a success story. Before he died Muhammad had unified Arabia,
made treaties with surrounding countries and established his
faith and followers on the world map. Within a century Islam
had spread into three continents – Africa, Asia and Europe.
Mecca and Medina are still the two most holy cities of Islam
and whatever happens in the Arabian heartlands affects
Muslims all over the world. Today the combination of religion,
politics and oil affect all humankind.

   The Arabia into which Muhammad was born was backward
and idolatrous. Animism, polytheism, female infanticide and
the oppression of women were widespread. Muslims refer to
this period as the age of ignorance. The country was populated
by nomadic and semi-nomadic desert tribes as well as by settled
city dwellers in towns like Mecca and Medina. Mecca was

both a commercial and pilgrimage centre. Among the numerous deities worshipped at Mecca were the three goddesses Mana, Al-Lat, and Al-Uzza. There were many tribal feuds and the country lacked unity. Arabia was affected by the power struggle between the Byzantine and Persian Empires.

Some Jewish communities lived in and around Mecca and Muhammad certainly came into contact with these, although he could not have read the Old Testament which had not been translated into Arabic. He probably also met Christians. The Hijaz near Mecca was the home of several nomadic Christian tribes. In the area of Yemen to the south there had been Christian tribes since the fourth century AD. In Mecca itself most of the Christians were foreigners. Muhammad may have met Syrian monks in the desert. The Christianity that Muhammad saw was a foreign religion. The New Testament was not translated into Arabic until after his death. Also the Christian Church was deeply divided by doctrinal disputes. Ever since the great Church Councils of Nicaea (325) and Chalcedon (451) the churches in the East had been arguing about the doctrines of the Trinity and the Person of Christ. The Monophysites emphasised Christ's divinity while giving the impression that he was not fully human. The Gnostics considered matter evil and denied his incarnation. So Muhammad may not have heard the true version of the Christian faith from those he met. Besides these problems with heresy, Christianity was heavily associated with political power and colonial expansion under the Byzantine emperors who were champions of the orthodox faith and fiercely repressed deviations from the religion of the state.

Into such a world Muhammad was born, in the tribe of Quraish, in the line of Abraham through his son Ishmael. Muhammad's father Abdullah died a few months before he was born and his mother died when he was only six years old. For the next two years until he also died his grandfather looked after him. Then his uncle Abu Talib took care of him. In 582 he began to accompany trading caravans into Syria where his earlier contacts with Jews and Christians in Mecca were reinforced. Eleven years later a wealthy widow called Khadija employed him in trading missions to Syria. In 595 at the age of twenty-five he married Khadija, thus gaining security and status.

His contacts with ascetics and monotheists called Hanifs led him to practise contemplation. In 610 at the age of forty he received his first 'revelation' in a cave on Mount Hira near Mecca. Eventually he was convinced that God was calling him to a special mission. He was visited in the cave by the Angel Gabriel with the message from God: 'Read . . .' (Q. 96:1–5).[1] His wife Khadija dispelled his self-doubts and became the first convert. Other family members, Zaid and Ali, followed, as did friends Abu Bakr and Umar. From 612 to 622 he preached in Mecca about belief in Allah and the Judgment Day (Q. 74:1–10), attracting persecution from his own tribe. Many of Muhammad's followers fled from Mecca and found refuge in the Christian kingdom of Abyssinia. In 617 the Muslims in Mecca were boycotted by their fellow Meccans. Personal sorrow added to Muhammad's burdens. His uncle Abu Talib died, and then his wife Khadija in 621. Khadija had been his only wife but now he contracted further marriages, thus strengthening his alliances with other Arabian tribes and also giving protection to war widows.

The content of his preaching focused on condemnation of idolatry and God's judgment on unbelief. He gained some followers from Medina, and the people of Medina invited him with his followers to come and be their leader. So in 622 the Hijrah took place and Islam was introduced to the world. Muhammad was now no longer the leader of a small persecuted band but a man of substance and importance. His authority increased. He became a spiritual leader, a legislator and a military commander for the new community. 'Revelations' dealt with matters of faith, rules about marriage and family life, war and booty, and laws for the community.

From 622 to 630 the main opposition continued to be from the Meccans. Other tribes were subjugated. He made forays against those who opposed him and raided passing caravans. In 624 Muhammad won the battle of Badr against the Meccans but the following year he lost the battle of Uhud against them. Accounts of the battle indicate that this defeat was related to the desertion of his Jewish supporters. In 627 he defended

Medina against attack in the battle of Ahzab. The next year the truce of Hudaibiya was made with the Meccans. These battles and the truce are described in the Quran. In 629 he massacred those Jews who opposed his teaching and sent out an 'Invitation' to surrounding rulers to accept Islam. The Chief of Bahrain accepted as did the Emperor of Abyssinia but the Byzantine Emperor refused.

In 630 Muhammad took Mecca as the Meccans had broken the treaty by attacking a tribe with whom he was in league. He destroyed the idols in the Kaaba (Q. 17:81). Then he won the battle of Hunian, distributing booty among the Meccans. When he returned to Medina delegations came from all over Arabia announcing acceptance of Islam. The next year he went on pilgrimage to Mecca (Q. 5:3) and delivered his Farewell Address. In 632 he fell ill, and died in Medina, probably on his sixty-third birthday. He was buried there.

To the Muslim Muhammad is both the greatest and the last of the prophets. Undoubtedly, Muhammad was an outstanding leader who has earned his place in world history. His courageous proclamation of the one God in an idolatrous society and his concern to improve the security of women and to prevent female infanticide are some of the evidences that he was a religious and moral reformer. He was a gifted military commander and a skilful statesman. Geoffrey Parrinder considers him to be a mystic. 'Unless mysticism is to be restricted to pantheism, then both by his religious experiences and by his teaching Muhammad qualifies as a mystic.'[2]

Not all have regarded him so positively. Al-Walid, an influential fellow-townsman of Muhammad, resolutely refused to acknowledge his claims. According to the traditions he discussed with pilgrims whether Muhammad should be regarded as a soothsayer or *kahin*, or as 'one possessed' (*majnun*), or as a poet. He himself would then conclude that it would perhaps be more correct to regard him as a magician or *sahir* (Q. 43:30–1; 74:21–5).[3]

Abu Bakr

No provision had been made for a successor to Muhammad. Abu Bakr, friend and early convert of Muhammad, succeeded him as the first Caliph (632–4), having been chosen by a small electoral body. The community ratified this choice, pledging loyalty to the new caliph. Abu Bakr's main achievement was to maintain the unity of the new Islamic state. Only a few tribes broke away. He also defeated the Byzantine army in the last year of his caliphate.

Unlike his successor, he tolerated those Christian communities in Arabia which submitted to his political authority.

Umar

Umar, the second Caliph (634–44), expelled all Christians from Arabia. Umar was another friend and early follower of Muhammad. He arranged for the collecting together of the sections of the Quran. He defeated the Byzantine army at the battle of Yarmuk. He captured Jerusalem, and gained control of Syria, Egypt and Persia.

Uthman

Uthman ruled as the third Caliph (644–56). He established the official text of the Quran and had other texts destroyed.

Ali

Ali, Muhammad's cousin and son-in-law, became the fourth Caliph (656–61). He had married Fatima, Muhammad's only daughter and surviving offspring. The Shia Muslims maintained that the true successor to Muhammad must be from his family so they discounted the preceding caliphs and accepted only Ali and his line.

Some Important Islamic Dynasties

Umayyad Dynasty (Sunnis), 661–750 in Damascus and 756–1031 in Spain

The Umayyad caliphs took the name of their dynasty from a Meccan ancestor of Muhammad called Umayya. From 661 to 750 the Umayyad dynasty ruled in Damascus, Syria. This was the Golden Age of Islam. Within a hundred years of Muhammad's death Islam had spread to three continents and ruled from Spain to Persia (Iran). Berber invasions from North Africa and Crusader pressure from Northern Spain caused the collapse of the Umayyads in Cordoba and its capture by Fernando III in 1236. The reconquest of Spain was completed when the last Moorish stronghold of Granada fell in 1492.

Abbasid Caliphate (Sunnis) of Baghdad, 750–1258

After leading a revolt against the Umayyads the Abbasid dynasty established its rule in Baghdad. Their caliphs descended directly from Abbas, an uncle of Muhammad. They claimed that they ruled by divine right, each naming himself 'God's shadow'. Their dynasty, weakened by internal corruption and opulence, fell before the Mongols who captured Baghdad in 1258. Salih al-Din had already ended the Shia Fatimid Caliphate in North Africa in 1169. The major centre of Muslim power shifted to the Ottoman Turks who ruled from 1517 to 1919. By far the most famous of them was Suleiman the Magnificent who ruled from 1520 to 1566 and controlled most of Hungary, South-Eastern Europe, North Africa and the Middle East. His capital was Byzantium, renamed Istanbul after the Turks captured it in 1453.

Fatimid Caliphate of North Africa, Egypt and Syria (Shias), 909–1171

The Fatimids claimed descent from Ali, the fourth Caliph, and took their name from his wife Fatima, the daughter of Muhammad. Their connection with the seventh imam Ismail has never been fully explained but they sustained the most successful and politically powerful achievements of the Ismailis branch of the Shias. Shia missionary activity prepared the

way in North Africa for the coming of the first Fatimid caliph,
Ubaydallah, who came from Syria. In 969 the Fatimid general
Jawhar captured Cairo. The Fatimids then began to build
their capital, New Cairo, called Al-Qahira 'the Victorious'.
When the Fatimid Empire began to crumble through internal
corruption and weakness Salih al-Din easily ended it in 1171.
The majority of the subjects of the Fatimids had remained
Sunnis. In 970 the Fatimids had founded the famous Al-Azhar
University to train Shia missionaries for work beyond their
empire. Economic prosperity together with extensive foreign
trade, cultural vitality and artist creativity marked the Fatimid
period before its declension and fall. Salih al-Din founded in
its place the Sunni Ayyubi dynasty (1171–1252) when the
Al-Azhar became Sunni, as it has remained to this day.

Abbasid Caliphate of Cairo, 1261–1517

When the last caliph of Baghdad was killed by the Mongol
invaders who reached Iraq and Syria, a survivor from his
family was made caliph in Cairo. However, the succession of
caliphs in Cairo had little power and were under the thumbs
of the Mamluk sultans of that city. The Mamluks were members of a military class descended from Turkish slaves. They
remained powerful in Egypt until the early nineteenth century.
During this Abbasid Caliphate Islam continued to spread,
reaching Indonesia and India.

Turkish-Ottoman Empire, 1517–1918

From Istanbul the Ottoman Turks advanced into Europe where
they held strongholds for four centuries. Twice they besieged
Vienna but failed to capture it. They were expelled from a
Polish province in the seventeenth century and later from
Greece and finally from the Balkans where nationalists fought
for independence in the nineteenth and beginning of the
twentieth century. The Ottoman Sultans of Istanbul took over
the title caliph after the conquest of Egypt in 1517. However,
with the emergence of the Turkish Republic the Caliphate
ended in 1924.

Religious Branches of Islam

Apart from the Sunni majority, religious groupings were often started by and then named after charismatic figures in Islam (see Fig. 1). There are three main groups in Islam: the Sunnis (almost 90 per cent of all Muslims), the Kharijis, otherwise known as Ibadis (a tiny minority), and the Shias (about 10 per cent). The divisions occurred over who should lead the Muslim community after the death of Muhammad. The Sunnis insisted on a descendant of the Arabian tribe of Muhammad, the Quraish. The Shias required a descendant of Muhammad himself, while the Kharijis declared that the head of the Muslim community must be the most worthy Muslim, regardless of whether he was Arab or not, a freeman or slave.

Sunnis

The Sunnis from the very beginning of historical Islam in 622 are the 'orthodox' Muslims who accept all the first four caliphs and the claims of the Umayyad Dynasty in Damascus to take over the caliphate with Muawiya as the first Umayyad caliph. Most of what will be described in Chapter 5 is Sunni teaching. While the Sunnis continue to be the largest grouping in Islam there are two main sub-groups: one small, the Kharijis, formed in 586, and the other much larger, dating from 661 – the Shias. All other groups are sub-groups of the Shias or have developed into their own world religion (the Bahais) or people community (the Druzes) or heretical group (the Ahmadis).

Kharijis (Ibadis)

The name Khariji means 'went out'. The Kharijis went out from the majority, separating themselves by rebelling. Ali was assassinated probably by discontented Khariji tribesmen, who started to dispute his authority in 656. This group or sect is closer to the Sunnis than to the Shias. Today Kharijis are now called Ibadis. The name Ibadi comes from the founder of a subsect of the Kharjis called Abdallah b. Ibad. Numbering about half a million they live in the Algerian Sahara, in Djerba (an island off Tunisia), in Tanzania and in the Sultanate of Oman and are few in number.

Fig.1. Historical Chart of Religious Branches in Islam

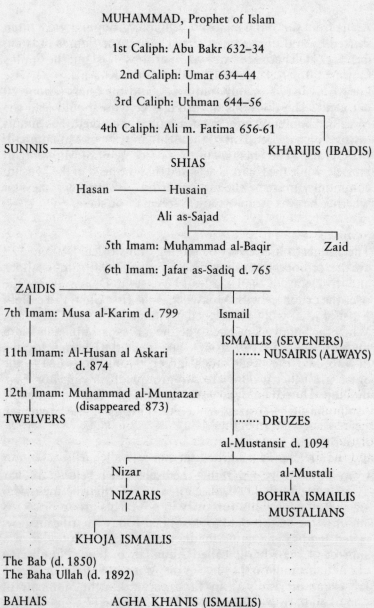

MUHAMMAD, Prophet of Islam

1st Caliph: Abu Bakr 632–34

2nd Caliph: Umar 634–44

3rd Caliph: Uthman 644–56

4th Caliph: Ali m. Fatima 656-61

SUNNIS ——————————————— KHARIJIS (IBADIS)

SHIAS

Hasan ———— Husain

Ali as-Sajad

5th Imam: Muhammad al-Baqir   Zaid

6th Imam: Jafar as-Sadiq d. 765

ZAIDIS ——————

7th Imam: Musa al-Karim d. 799   Ismail

ISMAILIS (SEVENERS)

11th Imam: Al-Husan al Askari   ······· NUSAIRIS (ALWAYS)
d. 874

12th Imam: Muhammad al-Muntazar
(disappeared 873)

TWELVERS   ······· DRUZES

al-Mustansir d. 1094

Nizar   al-Mustali

NIZARIS   BOHRA ISMAILIS
MUSTALIANS

KHOJA ISMAILIS

The Bab (d. 1850)
The Baha Ullah (d. 1892)

BAHAIS   AGHA KHANIS (ISMAILIS)

Shias or Twelvers

The battle of Karbala in 661 marks the beginning of Shia Islam. The name Shia is derived from an Arabic word meaning 'partisan'. Not all Shias agree on the number of imams or spiritual leaders. Those who agree on twelve are called 'Twelvers' and those who agree on seven are called 'Seveners'. Shia majorities are found in Iran (90 per cent), Iraq, Bahrain, and the Eastern province of Saudi Arabia. These wealthy oil-rich areas have attracted much world attention in the last two decades, through the Khomeini-inspired revolution in Iran, the struggle for control of the Arabian/Persian Gulf in the Iran-Iraq War, and the invasion of Kuwait by Saddam Hussein with the ensuing Gulf War. All these economic and political dangers have focused attention on the Shias and their distinctive beliefs and practices. The largest Shia minorities are in Pakistan (10 per cent), India and Lebanon (nearly 50 per cent). Shia Islam has sub-divided into many groups. This is partly because of the Shia emphasis on charismatic leaders.

The Shia movement started as a group aiming to restore the caliphate to Ali and his descendants. The Shias recognised twelve imams. In 873 the last imam (twelfth or seventh according to the group) mysteriously vanished. They believe he will return at the end of time to become the head of the community. Since then they have awaited the return of this Hidden Imam. An imam is regarded as a charismatic and infallible leader. They hold a non-literal and sometimes esoteric interpretation of the Quran. They expect salvation through the messianic return of the Mahdi or 'Guided One'. The tombs of the imams, especially that of Husain, are major shrines and the first ten days of the first month, called Muharram, is a major religious observance. The Shias have attracted non-Arabs who have felt excluded from power. Shia Islam became the dominant religious affiliation of Iran in the sixteenth century and remains so today.

Ismailis or Sevener Shias

The term Sevener Shia gives the impression that the group deals with a line of only seven imams. This was certainly the case to start with, but it has since divided and some groups recognise a continued line of imams. The present Agha Khan is considered by his followers to be the forty-ninth imam. The name Ismaili refers to Ismail, the son of the Imam Jafar al-Sadiq. Although he died before his father in 755 all Ismaili groups recognise him to be the former's rightful successor, and continue the line of imams from him. Ismail is not, as is often maintained, the seventh imam, but the sixth because the Ismailis attribute a special role to Ali and begin the line of imams with Ali's son, Hasan. They regard Ismail's son Muhammad as the seventh imam, with whom the line originally ended.

In a mere twenty-five years up to 900, the Ismaili mission formed a network of communities spanning the whole Islamic world from North Africa to India. The Ismaili imam claimed understanding of the hidden inner sense of Quranic revelation and taught that all details of the secret doctrine are to be found encoded in the Quran. The method of reading this secret sense from the text of the Quran is called 'interpretation'.

During the imamate of the Fatimids the jurist and chief judge al-Numan ibn Muhammad al-Tamimi (d. 974) founded the Ismaili legal school with his compendium *The Pillars of Islam* and at the same time revealed the secret sense of legal and cultic prescriptions in several other works. Cairo under the Fatimids became the centre of Ismaili mission. The Fatimids did not force their Sunni subjects to adopt the Ismaili faith, but numerous conversions resulted from their missionary enterprise.

Zaidis

The Zaidis, recognising only the first four imams, are a group which broke off after the death of the fourth imam. They claim that the fifth imam should not have been Muhammad al-Baqir but rightfully his brother Zaid who was martyred during the reign of the Umayyad Caliph Hisham. Today the Zaidis number about four million and are mostly found in the north of Yemen where half the population is Zaidi. They have been without a religious leader since 1962 and are doctrinally the most liberal of the Shias, having been influenced by the rationalist Mutazilites. They reject the idea of the Hidden

Imam and any mystical approaches to religion.

Nizaris or Assassins

After the death of Caliph al-Mustansir in 1094 his son Nizar established himself in the fortress of Alamut, but he was defeated and executed by a rival. This coup caused the Iranian followers of Nizar to defect under the leadership of Hasan-i Sabbah. He became the founder of the 'Assassins', who moved around in small groups calling themselves the 'ones prepared to sacrifice themselves' because they usually met their deaths in terrorist operations. When Hasan-i Sabbah died in 1124 he was succeeded first by Buzurg-Ummid, whom he had designated himself and who in turn appointed his son Muhammad to be his successor. He thus founded a dynasty which ruled over the small Ismaili state of Alamut and castles in Syria and eastern Iran for more than a century. The Nizari Ismailis gained new impetus under Buzurg-Ummid's grandson Hasan II (1162–6). He declared a new era and that Islamic law, which had until then been scrupulously observed, was annulled at the bidding of the Hidden Imam. After a sermon in the courtyard of Alamut castle to an assembled crowd which turned its back to Mecca, he invited the audience to a feast in the middle of the fast of Ramadan.

In this barely accessible mountain region the 'Assassins' established a small territorial state like that of Alamut and pursued a clever seesaw policy in the border area between the Crusader states of the coast and the Seljuq emirates of Aleppo and Damascus. The most famous prince of the Syrian Assassin state was Rashid al-Din Sinan, called 'the old man from the mountains' by the Crusaders. His most dangerous opponent was Sultan Salih al-Din (Saladin) who overthrew the Fatimid dynasty in Cairo and extended his rule to Syria.

In 1964 the number of Ismailis in Syria was 56,000, 1 per cent of the total population.

Khoja Ismailis

The other imami line can be traced from the end of the fifteenth century in the village of Anjudan near Mahallat (100 km south-west of Qumm). It is said to be descended from the great

Masters of Alamut, and is the so-called Qasim-Shahi line to which today's Agha Khan belongs. After a failed rebellion attempt in Kirman the first Agha Khan had to flee to Afghanistan in 1842. Three years later he finally settled in Bombay. The communities of the Nizari-Ismailis in North-West India, the Khojas (from Persian *khwaja* meaning master), developed when a Hindu trader caste was converted to Islam. Even today the Khojas are almost exclusively traders.

The number of imami Khojas amounts to about twenty million, of whom some two million are in Pakistan where numerous Khojas settled after being expelled from Uganda in 1972. Karachi has superseded Bombay as the most important community on the subcontinent.

Agha Khanis

The father of the first Agha Khan, Khalilullah, a villager from near the Persian city of Qumm, was revered by his followers as divine. His son became the governor of Mahallat and Qumm, receiving the title of Agha Khan (Turkish for 'prince') from the Shah. When he was compelled to flee to India he joined his Khoja followers. The Agha Khans are still regarded as incarnations of the divine. The third Agha Khan was a reformer who promoted monogamy, opposed the seclusion of women and through his economic programmes enabled his followers to become a wealthy business community. His grandson the present Agha Khan, Karim Hazar, a Pakistani citizen, is an outstanding leader not only for his own people but in his work when head of the United Nations High Commission for Refugees. The Agha Khanis founded the modern Agha Khan University in Karachi. Their work in the deprived Northern Areas of Pakistan, where they run schools and clinics, is impressive. Teachers and nurses from Karachi go for voluntary two-year stints to help the less privileged members of their community.

Mustalians or Bohras

Not all Ismailis are followers of the Agha Khan. Many Khojas do not recognise him nor do the descendants of the Fatimid Caliph Mustali. An Indian caste of traders embraced the faith and became known as Bohras or Bohoras. A split about leadership resulted in the formation of two groups. Together they number about half a million of whom around 3,000 live in the United Kingdom. They are clearly within the Shia religious tradition but are secretive about their beliefs. They pray three times a day, do not assemble on Fridays but use the normal pattern of Islamic ritual prayer.

Nusairis or Alawis

The name Nusairi is derived from a Syrian coastal mountain range called Jabal (mountain) al-Nusairiyya. Present-day Nusairis, an offshoot of Ismaili missionary activity, deify Ali, claiming he sent Muhammad as Prophet. They hold a reinterpretation of Husain's martyrdom believing that he was not actually killed at the battle of Karbala but that it only appeared so. (All Shias consider Husain's death a martyrdom.) The Nusairis also interpret Quranic revelation and Islamic law 'spiritually'. Members of the sect have held the most important positions in Syria ever since the coup of the Nusairi head of the Air Force, now President Hafiz al-Asad, in 1970. Today they dominate the country through their 600,000 members, although they only make up about 11 per cent of the population. In order to repudiate the accusation of heresy the Nusairis have from the beginning of the present century called themselves 'Alawis', i.e. Ali supporters or Shias. Some live in Turkey.

Ahmadis

The name Ahmadi is taken from the founder Hazrat Mirza Ghulam Ahmad, born in Qadian in the Indian Punjab in 1835, who established his movement in 1889 to reaffirm and renew Islam. He claimed to be the Messiah mentioned in the Bible and in Quranic prophecies and regarded himself as the Restorer (or Mahdi) of Islam expected towards the beginning of the new Islamic century. His claim to prophethood is rejected by orthodox Muslims who consider Ahmadis heretical. Ghulam Ahmad Mirza taught that Jesus did not die on the cross but only swooned and that he lived to be 120 years old and is buried in Kashmir. After the founder's death in 1908 the movement split in two over whether he was or was not a prophet. The breakaway group with headquarters in Lahore acknowledged him as a reformer but not a prophet. Both groups consider themselves Ahmadis but the Lahore branch are called Lahoris and they call the other branch Qadianis (from the village where their founder was born) or Mirzais (from another of his names). The 1974 Conference of World Muslim Organisations in Mecca declared them unacceptable and urged individual nations to declare Ahmadis in their respective countries as non-Muslims. Pakistan, with over a million Ahmadis, did this later in that year. The movement proselytises vigorously and is worldwide but is especially active in Africa and Indonesia. Ahmadis total about twelve million in all.

Druzes

Hamza, a Persian from eastern Iran, was the real founder of Druzism. His letters form part of the holy canon of Druze documents. He taught that the Fatimid al-Hakim (d. 1021), whom he regarded as the Hidden Imam, was divine; that the Quran and its Ismaili interpretation were abrogated and replaced by the simple confession of God's unity. This made all cultic acts irrelevant. One of Hamza's supporters, a young Turk called al-Darzi (Persian, the tailor), became so active a missionary that followers of the new doctrine were named Darzis or Druzes (*Duruz*, pl. of *Darzi*) after him. Even today the writings of Hamza are only accessible to a minority of initiated scholars who study the writings every Thursday in secluded cells in the mountains. The majority do not know the secrets of their own religion. Under such circumstances the Druze doctrine did not continue to develop, and so for centuries the Druzes have been a distinctive social community. It now numbers about a quarter of a million, confined mainly to Lebanon, Syria and Israel. The Druzes are not regarded as Muslims despite their Ismaili origins.

Bahais

In the twentieth century Bahaism has developed into an independent religion with a universal claim and a worldwide mission so it can no longer be described as a Shia sect. Bahais can no longer be regarded as Muslim. Due to its organised missionary activity there are now Bahai communities in 139 countries. About half a million Bahais live in Iran but their headquarters is now in Haifa, Israel. This movement was first planted in 1844 in Iran by a Persian teacher of religion who called himself the Bab (literally 'gate'). His disciples further developed it, calling themselves Babis. After the execution of the Bab for heresy in 1850 one of his disciples Baha Ullah was accepted as the leader and his Babi followers changed their name to Bahais in his honour. Bahaism now claims to be the fulfilment of all previous religions and uses simplified Islamic ritual. Until the present day Bahais have experienced persecution. For example, in 1955 the Shah allowed the *ulama* a free hand against the sect. Their dome in Tehran was pulled down with the Shah's consent and the army's co-operation. Calls to the people to oppose the Bahais had previously been transmitted by national radio. The Shah, however, successfully resisted the *ulama*'s demands to outlaw all Bahais and seize their property.

Two Outstanding Personalities in the History of Islam

Al-Ghazali

Probably the most famous religious personality of the Middle Ages was Al-Ghazali (1058–1111), Persian theologian, philosopher and mystic, considered by some to be the greatest Muslim since Muhammad. Al-Ghazali was a professor of Theology and Law in Baghdad but being spiritually unsatisfied, he turned to Islamic mysticism. He left his teaching work and travelled to holy places and retreat centres to look for further light on the mystic or Sufi path. This is how he describes his spiritual pilgrimage which encompassed both traditional theology and mystical experience: 'I saw clearly that the mystics were men of personal experience not of words, and I had gone as far as possible by way of study and intellectual application, so that only personal experience and walking in the mystic way were left.'[4] This fusion probably made him generally acceptable, bringing a respectability to Sufism which had seemed outside the main stream of Islam. One of his most famous writings is *Miskat al Anwar* in which he expounds the mystical meaning of the famous Light verse (Q. 24:35):

> Allah is the Light of the heavens and the earth. The similitude of His light is as a niche wherein is a lamp. The lamp is in a glass. The glass is as it were a shining star. (This lamp is) kindled from a blessed tree, an olive neither of the East nor of the West, whose oil would almost glow forth (of itself) though no fire touched it. Light upon light. Allah guideth unto His light whom He will. And Allah speaketh to mankind in allegories, for Allah is Knower of all things.

Like many Sufis, al-Ghazali exhibited tolerance and understanding of Christians.

Muhammad Iqbal

Muhammad Iqbal (1849–1938) of India is one of the most influential modern personalities of Islam. Like Muhammad Abduh of Egypt (1849–1905) he helped to show his fellow Muslims the relevance of Islam to the modern world.

Muhammad Iqbal, through his Urdu and Persian poetry, and through his English lectures entitled *Reconstruction of Religious Thought in Islam,* became the poet philosopher of the Indian subcontinent and the patron saint of Pakistan which he dreamed of but never lived to see. On 28 May 1937 he wrote to Muhammad Ali Jinnah who was to become the first Governor General of Pakistan at its creation in 1947: 'The enforcement and development of the Shariat of Islam is impossible in this country without a free Muslim state or states.' He was a visionary rather than a politician. Through his philosophy, expressed in verse as well as prose, he analysed the condition of the modern world. Returning to Lahore after studies in Munich and Cambridge he became a professor and then a barrister. He taught that self or 'ego' could only reach fulfilment by effort and mastery over the world. So freedom was based on monotheism, prophethood, a code (the Quran), a centre (Mecca) and the clear objective of disseminating the doctrine of the unity of God. His ideal society must gain supremacy over the natural world and must safeguard motherhood. These concepts revitalised Islam in the subcontinent and inspired Muslims to seek an independent Muslim homeland. Iqbal is still deeply respected and his poetry widely read not only in the Islamic Republic of Pakistan but in Bangladesh and among the world's largest Muslim minority of more than a hundred million in India.

1. In all instances Q. is used as an abbreviation for Quran. The first number shows the number of the surah or chapter of the Quran and the following number or numbers indicate the particular verses. Thus, Q. 96:1–5 indicates Quran surah 96 verses 1–5.
2. *Mysticism in the World's Religions* (Sheldon Press, 1976), pp. 127–8.
3. See D. M. Donaldson, *Studies in Muslim Ethics,* (SPCK, 1963), p. 38.
4. W. Montgomery Watt, *Muslim Intellectual: A Study of Al-Ghazali* (Edinburgh University Press, 1953), p. 135.

3

The Community of the Faithful

This chapter deals with the geographical spread of Islam, first the religious, intellectual and economic centres of Islam, and then the various countries where Muslims are at present a majority or a significant minority. There are ethnic groups and tribes which are almost entirely Muslim, like the Baluchis, the Pathans which are divided between two countries and the Uighurs who form the largest of the Muslim minorities in one province in China.

Centres of Islam

Saudi Arabia

Whatever happens in the heartlands of Islam affects Muslims all over the world. Saudi Arabia is the religious centre of Islam with the two most holy cities – Mecca and Medina. The King of Saudi Arabia is the Custodian of the Two Holy Mosques, King Fahd ibn Abdul Aziz Al Saud, Imam and Protector of the Faith. Increasing numbers of Muslims come from every continent and many lands each year on pilgrimage. The unifying effect of this experience and the other opportunities it offers for international exchange increase year by year. Modern travel and developing facilities within Saudi Arabia have brought an annual increase in the number of pilgrims to the present estimate of well over two million a year.

Islam is the official religion of the Kingdom of Saudi Arabia and all Saudi citizens must be Muslims. Apostasy is a crime punishable by death. No non-Muslim places of worship are permitted anywhere in the country.

Egypt

Egypt, especially Cairo with the Al-Azhar University, is the intellectual centre of Islam. There Muslim missionaries from many countries are trained and then return to spread the faith in their own countries. The widening of the Al-Azhar syllabus and the increase of faculties in 1961 has made it one of the largest and most modern universities in Egypt. Many Muslim professionals are trained there. (It is not open to Copts.) After qualifying at the Al-Azhar many Egyptians and those of other nationalities then take jobs abroad, particularly in other Arab countries. The influence of Cairo and the Al-Azhar goes out through people, radio, TV, cassette and the printed word to the twenty-one Arabic-speaking countries of the Middle East, but the ripples are felt far beyond the Arab world.

Gulf states

Muslims view their oil wealth as the blessing of Allah. The economic development accompanying the discovery of so much oil has resulted in the temporary migration of millions of people. Arabs from poorer Arab lands flock to the oil lands of the Middle East. The influx in the late sixties and seventies of Indians, Pakistanis and Bangladeshis from the subcontinent, followed by Koreans and Filipinos in the eighties, was unprecedented. Some oil states, notably Qatar and the United Arab Emirates, have drawn over three-quarters of their work force from abroad, even though there is now a stress on indigenisation.

Six of the oil states, Kuwait, Qatar, Saudi Arabia, the United Arab Emirates, Bahrain and the Sultanate of Oman have formed the Gulf Cooperation Council (GCC). All these countries are monarchical, ruled by a king, sultan, emir or sheikh. The fact that the rulers are all Sunnis (except the Sultan of Oman who is Ibadi) and that a considerable number of their subjects are Shia accounts for a certain amount of recent unrest, especially in Bahrain. For Saudi Arabia, estimates of

Shias fluctuate but a realistic figure would be about 350,000 (6 per cent). The Shias live almost exclusively in the Eastern Province and comprise around half of all workers in the oilfields. Of the Saudi indigenous population about 79 per cent are Sunni of Wahhabi persuasion. All the Gulf states have Shia minorities: in Kuwait and Qatar about 20 per cent, in the United Arab Emirates 7 per cent, but in Oman only 0.1 per cent. In Bahrain the majority is Shia – about 70 per cent.

The Gulf War of 1991 has changed many things but a desire for reform has been in the air in the Gulf states for a long time, certainly since oil production became viable. In Kuwait the division over social customs is perhaps a greater post-war issue than the economic reconstruction of the Emirate. The latter is predictable but it is the former that could divide the country. Over 300,000 Kuwaitis fled the country when Iraq invaded. The majority went to Saudi Arabia. Some returned more conservative in their views on social affairs, even desiring to install religious police (like those in Saudi Arabia) responsible for ensuring that everyone obeys Islamic customs of modesty and avoids alcohol. Those Kuwaitis who fled to the West are on the whole more liberal than previously. They want personal freedom to be able to make their own choices.

In Saudi Arabia women are not allowed to pray in mosques, with the exception of the mosques in Mecca and Medina. The Saudi government does not allow Saudi women, irrespective of age or status, to travel abroad outside the Kingdom without the written permission of a male 'guardian'. Women may hold more liberal views but without male support or revolution their emancipation might be slow. Soraya Altorki's recent study of ideology and behaviour among thirteen elite families in Jiddah through three generations highlights dramatic changes in society. She comments that there are more nuclear than extended families, and that there is more interaction socially between husband and wife, more private education and overseas travel, and mutual consultation on domestic matters such as the education of children.[1] In general we can expect more radical changes in the position and role of women in the GCC countries.

Widespread education in these lands has been a dramatic factor in change. For example, education is fairly new for both girls and boys in the Sultanate of Oman. Its first, and at present only, university was founded in 1986 with five faculties. Women students have been in the majority from the start of Sultan Qaboos University. Nevertheless, only about 9 per cent civil servants are women and the percentage of female employees is much less in the private sector where expatriate secretaries and teachers are often preferred. However, an increasing stress on 'Omanisation' may change this. The state religion of the Sultanate is Ibadi Islam to which about 84 per cent of the population adhere.

Pakistan

When we turn from the heartlands of Islam and the Middle East where three great religions and continents meet, our gaze should follow that of the Muslim to Pakistan 'the land of the pure'. As Bishop Kenneth Cragg has said: 'Pakistan, as concept, policy and fact, must be seen as the surest Muslim index to Islam in our time, doing for its contemporary definition what the Hijra did in the seventh century.'[2]

Pakistan is a twentieth-century Islamic experiment, the success of which is very important to Muslims everywhere. To sustain its sagging economy Saudi Arabia pours in aid. A state founded in the name of Islam must not fail. Its greatest crisis came in the civil war of 1971 when it became evident that the two wings of Pakistan, divided by nearly a thousand miles of hostile Indian territory, could not survive. Out of this agony East Pakistan became Bangladesh. The nightmare still haunts Pakistan. If one part of the country can drop off what about other parts? The early governments of Pakistan were content to maintain the country rather than define it but President Zia ul-Haq started to define what a Muslim state is. He began by introducing *Nizam-e-Mustafa* i.e. the organisation of society according to the way of the Prophet of Islam. (Mustafa is one of Muhammad's names.) Muslim banking was introduced, forbidding usury. Arabic became the second language of state schools in place of English. Women faced more restrictions and certain matters came under

the newly introduced Shariat Bench Ordinance. The next
governments under Nawaz Sharif and Benazir Bhutto tried
to please the more liberal sections of society as well as the
fundamentalists. However, Shariah law was further extended
and the minorities began to feel more threatened. In 1991 a
second modified Shariah Bill became law but it did not allay
fears about the position of women and minorities. Also in
1991 the Blasphemy Law or *Gustakh-e-Rasool,* introduced
in 1986, was amended by the Federal Shariah Court to make
the death penalty mandatory for anyone convicted of blasphemy (directly or indirectly, by word, gesture, innuendo or
otherwise defiling the name of the Prophet Muhammad). The
Federal Shariah Court brought in this amendment in
accordance with its constitutional obligation to amend any
law to the extent that it has been found un-Islamic.

Bangladesh

Bangladesh is 86 per cent Muslim while Pakistan is 95 per
cent Muslim. In March 1988 Islam became the state religion
of Bangladesh. Like Pakistan it also elected a woman Prime
Minister. In Bangladesh, as in Pakistan, about 70 per cent of
the Muslims go to shrines or belong to religious brotherhoods.
The most famous of these orders are the Chisti, the
Naqshbandi, the Surhawardi and the Qadiri. One can call
this popular or folk religion. It tends to revolve round a particular saint and shrine. The Surhawardi order, for example,
was introduced by Shaikh Bahauddin Zakariya. He died in
1266 and his tomb, shrine and mosque complex in Multan,
Pakistan, is constantly visited by devotees. Popular or folk
religion of this sort is denounced by the fundamentalists,
especially by the Wahhabis, a missionary reform movement
founded and based in Saudi Arabia, and by Jamaat-i-Islami
members, of whom we will learn more later.

Afghanistan

Afghanistan, having been strongly Muslim for so many
centuries, is not so consciously Muslim as the newly created
states of Pakistan and Bangladesh. The communist influence
in recent years has probably reduced the number of those

practising folk Islam. If it is able to re-establish its viability as a country and become politically stable Afghanistan will become an important crossroads for trade and Islam between Pakistan and the new Muslim republics of Central Asia. The largest ethnic groups of Afghanistan, the Pathans, Tajiks and Uzbeks, are Hanafi Sunnis. Only about 6 per cent of the population is Shia.

Turkey

Turkey is a secular state with a 99 per cent Muslim population made up of 85 per cent Sunni and 14 per cent Alawi Shia. The latter are mainly Kurds. The Kurds are the largest ethnic group in the world without a country of their own. They are an ancient people (Salih al-Din was a Kurd), nearly all Muslims, speaking different Kurdish dialects and spread over Turkey, Iran, Iraq, Syria and the former USSR. Most Kurds are Sunnis but in Iran 25 per cent are Shia and in Turkey and Syria they follow the Alawi subsect of the Shias.

Kemal Ataturk made far-reaching reforms when he founded the Turkish Republic as a secular state in 1923 after the dismemberment of the Ottoman Empire. In recent years the revival of Muslim fundamentalism has strongly influenced Turkey as the fundamentalists have gathered political strength. The country has remained a secular state with a constitution that guarantees freedom of religion. It should be noted that Kemalist ideology rejected the role of Islam in politics and culture. Kemal envisioned the Turks as a European people in a secular state. Minorities differing in ethnicity and language and sometimes religion have continued to be just as disadvantaged as they were under the Ottoman regime. For Orthodox Christians emigration has been the main answer. For the Kurds conflict within the country continues. Human rights have been a continuing issue as secular Turkey struggles with its own identity under fundamentalist resurgence.

Iran

Iran is 98 per cent Muslim. Nine out of every ten Iranians are Shia. After the revolution the Islamic Constitution was formulated by an Assembly of Experts, most of whom were mullahs, in December 1979. Article 26 states: 'Parties, groups, political and professional associations, as well as Islamic or recognised minority religious associations are permitted, provided they do not violate principles of independence, freedom and national unity, or which are not contrary to the principles of Islam . . . or the Islamic Republic.' The legal situation with regard to religious freedom was radically altered, especially in the case of Iranians who adopted the Christian faith.

Just before the revolution many women adopted the veil or chadar as a political symbol of disapproval for the Shah and his regime or from fear of fundamentalists. (There were stories of women having acid thrown in their faces which, true or not, frightened women.) After the revolution Ayatollah Khomeini called for all women to return to wearing it. However, in 1979, some of these same women, wearing Western dress, marched on International Women's Day to protest against the Ayatollah's pronouncements on women's role in society. This brought some greater freedom but it did not last long.

Kazakhstan, Uzbekistan, Tajikistan, Kyrgyzstan and Turkmenistan

These are five of the Commonwealth of Independent States, formerly part of the USSR. Of the fifty-two million Muslims in the former USSR forty million, mainly Sunnis, live in these new republics. Their territorial area is five times larger than France. In the present unstable political climate, Islamic fundamentalism has a strong appeal for some Muslims, but most advocate the secular Turkish model. Kazakhstan and Kyrgyzstan have secular governments.

Indonesia

Indonesia is the largest Muslim country in the world as far as population is concerned (more than 80 per cent of its 187 million people are Muslim) but Islam is not the state religion. Indonesia is a secular republic. The Constitution of Indonesia provides conditions for religious peace and freedom by acknowledging equal rights for Islam, the Catholic Church, the Protestant Church, Buddhism and Hinduism. Every citizen is required to belong to one of these five recognised religious systems. Members of all the five religious systems have the same right and duty to participate in the political, social and economic life of the nation.

Islam in Indonesia has been strongly influenced by popular religious beliefs and practices including Javanese mysticism, animism, and Hinduised Islam which came centuries ago from India. Orthodox Indonesian Muslims are very critical of this folk Islam. Muslim modernists have tried to purify Indonesian Islam by rejecting Sufism and visits to the tombs of saints. In Indonesia the divorce rate is unusually high at 52 per cent of marriages. Indonesia is the only country in the modern era where large numbers of people from Muslim backgrounds have joined the Christian churches.

The Maghrib or North-West Africa

In Arabic Maghrib literally means 'the West'. It includes Morocco, Algeria, Tunisia and Libya. It is well to remember that over 60 per cent of the entire population of the Maghrib is under twenty-five. The main ideological struggle is between secular humanism and Islamic fundamentalism. Secular humanism is linked to the French language as the main vehicle of European culture while the fundamentalist influences come from Egypt and are linked to Arabic. In Algeria this current of Islamic fundamentalism has grown stronger and politically powerful through the Islamic Salvation Front. In the kingdom of Morocco Islam is the state religion. Under the Constitution non-Muslims are guaranteed freedom of religion (Article 220–3) but generally this is applied only to expatriates. Morocco has a dual legal system. The secular system is partly based on the French legal tradition while an Islamic system decides on family matters and inheritance laws for Muslims, who comprise 99 per cent of the population.

Sudan

Sudan has an Islamic government. It is 74 per cent Muslim, made up of Sunnis belonging to powerful Sufi brotherhoods. Almost all Northern Sudan is Muslim. In 1983 President

Nimeiri, under pressure from groups like the Muslim Brotherhood, proclaimed the Shariah as the supreme law of the state and himself as imam. The predominant Islamic school of law is that of Sunni Maliki, by which the husband is recognised as head of the family with rights of control over his wife's property and children. Traditional Sudanese society is male-orientated. The Constitution proclaims equality between men and women and forbids any discrimination among Sudanese citizens 'on the basis of birth, religion, race or sex'. Nevertheless, the inequality between the sexes in the economic, social, political and family levels is striking. The attempt to impose Shariah in the South, where there are considerable Christian settlements, was one factor leading to the terrible civil war which is still not resolved. The law on apostasy has been applied to political dissidents (Mahmoud Mohamed Taha in 1985) and to converts from Islam to Christianity (Abdalla Yousef in 1994). Section 126 of the 1991 Penal Code mandates the death penalty for apostasy that 'is committed by any Muslim who advocates apostasy from Islam or openly declares his [her] own apostasy expressly or by categorical action'.

Muslims in Minority

Nigeria

One African in every five is Nigerian. Nigeria, the most populous country in Africa, is 45 per cent Muslim. The Northern provinces of Nigeria have experienced a long exposure to Arab and Muslim influence. The question of the future orientation of Nigerian society has especially focused round the debate over the membership of Nigeria in the Organisation of the Islamic Conference (OIC), an international political organisation which brings together almost all the Muslim-majority nation-states, and the inclusion of Shariah in the Constitution of the country. After a period of observer status and as a member for a few years the Nigerian Government suspended its membership of the OIC in 1992, partly because of concern expressed by its majority Christian population. At the present time Shariah is included in the Constitution but applies only to Muslims.

India

India has the largest Muslim minority in the world – over a hundred million, about 12 per cent of the total population, accessible but often forgotten. Many Indian Muslims speak Urdu at home but find it difficult to write it as it is not a state language (except in Jammu and Kashmir), so Hindi, English and the state language take precedence over Urdu in the schools. Muslims are found mainly in the following states: Jammu and Kashmir with 64 per cent of the state population; Assam with 24 per cent; Kerala with 21 per cent; Uttar Pradesh with 16 per cent and West Bengal with 21 per cent.

Philippines

The Philippines have a population of sixty-five million people, 8.4 per cent of whom are Muslims. They live mostly in South-West Mindanao and use a variety of languages. The 'militant' liberation organisations among them engage in anti-government activities, kidnapping and other forms of terrorism. Most Filipino Muslims, realising that they are unlikely to be able to integrate with or secede from the majority of their fellow-citizen Filipinos, would probably be satisfied with well-structured autonomy within the Republic of the Philippines.

North-West China

In China Muslims form 2.4 per cent of the population. Out of fifty-five ethnic minorities ten are Muslim and number about twenty-seven million. Nine of these minorities reside in the autonomous region of Sinkiang in North-West China. The most numerous are the Uighurs at about 6,660,000 people and then the Kazakhs with a million. The eight million Hui Chinese Muslims are spread all over China. With 14,000 functioning mosques Islam is one of the resurgent faiths filling the present spiritual vacuum. Communism has given Muslim women in China a greater sense of worth, independence and equality with men.

South America
In South America Muslims only exist in minority, the largest
group being in Brazil which has about 147,400 mainly Arab
Muslims, equalling 0.15 per cent of the total population.

United States of America
The present two and a half million Muslims are steadily
increasing through immigration (Iranians) and conversion of
Black Americans to Islam. Approximately 120,000 overseas
Muslims are studying in USA.

United Kingdom
Over 2 per cent of the population, about one million people,
are Muslim, predominantly from South Asia but with some
Arabs, Turks, Iranians etc. The Muslim communities have
grown rapidly through immigration, and a high birth-rate.
About 5,000 people have converted to Islam and there are
20,000 students from overseas. There are 1,200 mosques
(registered and unregistered) and 3,000 Quranic schools in
the UK and an increasing number of highly organised
communities which press for legislation to help their causes.

Other groupings
While we think of Muslim minority groups like the ones
mentioned above we should not forget the other groupings
of Muslims in minority – Muslim students studying outside
their own countries (e.g. 120,000 in the USA), wealthy Arab
tourists in the capitals of Europe, Muslim refugees whether
from Afghanistan, Iran, Bosnia or elsewhere. Then there are
the Muslim migrants and immigrants who have sought and
found work abroad, such as Turkish 'guest workers' in
Germany and Holland or North Africans in France. Also in
the West, as in Korea, there are citizens who have become
Muslims. Finally there is the growing number of Muslim
citizens in such countries whose children and grandchildren
are born Muslim. Muslims tend to have large families and so
the growth rate among Muslims is generally higher than among
many other groups.

Conclusion

Muslims now number about one billion. They comprise a majority in thirty-seven nations and have significant and growing minorities in many more. Sociologically, they include some of the richest and poorest communities in the world. Ethnic dispersion is considerable in response to trade, war and emigration.

1. Soraya Altorki, *Women in Saudi Arabia: Ideology and Behavior among the Elite* (Columbia University Press, 1986).

2. *Counsels in Contemporary Islam* (Edinburgh University Press, 1965), p. 29.

4

Sacred Texts

The Holy Quran

An eternal book
Muslims believe that the Quran is an eternal book. The original is written on 'a guarded tablet' (Q. 85:21) in heaven in Arabic. 'Lo, We have made it an Arabic Quran, mayhap ye will understand, and lo, it is in the Mother of the Book in Our presence, exalted, wise' (Q. 43:2–3).[1]

Revealed to the Prophet Muhammad
The first part of the Quran descended on the Night of Power (Q. 97:1) in the month of Ramadan: 'The month of Ramadan in which was revealed the Quran, a guidance for mankind, and clear proofs of the guidance, and the Criterion (of right and wrong) . . .' (Q. 2:185). It was revealed piece by piece to the Prophet Muhammad. 'And (it is) a Quran that We have divided, that thou mayest recite it unto mankind at intervals, and We have revealed it by (successive) revelation' (Q. 17:106) and 'But for the grace of Allah upon thee (Muhammad), and His mercy, a party of them had resolved to mislead thee, but they will mislead only themselves and they will hurt thee not at all. Allah revealeth unto thee the Scripture and wisdom, and teacheth thee that which thou knewest not . . .' (Q. 4:113). The Angel Gabriel – Jibrail in Arabic – was considered the agent for conveying the revelation to Muhammad (Q. 2:97).

Compiled by followers

Some of Muhammad's followers memorised the revelations he recited. During his lifetime some of the revelations were probably written down by his followers or by secretaries. According to a highly attested tradition Umar, seeing that many of the memorisers had been killed in battle, urged the first Caliph Abu Bakr to make a complete collection of the revelations in writing. Eventually Abu Bakr commissioned one of Muhammad's secretaries called Zayd ibn Thabit to do this. The tradition said he collected the verses 'from pieces of papyrus, flat stones, palm leaves, shoulder blades and ribs of animals, pieces of leather and wooden boards as well as from the hearts of men' to form the whole Quran. The third Caliph Uthman commissioned Zayd ibn Thabit to standardise the text by always using the dialect of the Quraish whenever there was a variant reading. This became the authoritative text and all others were to be destroyed.

The Quran, the greatest miracle

To obtain some appreciation of what the Quran means to the Muslim, we ought to hear it recited in Arabic. The Quran was revealed in Arabic, therefore the Arabic of the Quran is an essential part of its message. Part of the appeal for the Muslim lies in the cadence and beauty of the Arabic. The Quran is regarded as the greatest miracle of all in that it is a lasting miracle, revealed in superb poetry and language to a relatively uneducated and possibly illiterate man. Muhammad is described as *ummi* (variously translated 'unlearned' or 'illiterate') in the Quran (7:157).

Translations?

Translating the Arabic into other languages has generally been discouraged. Today, however, translations are being allowed, and some have the approval of Muslim leaders. They are regarded as paraphrases and have been given titles like *The Koran Interpreted* (A. J. Arberry). The Quran is only the Quran in Arabic: 'I have given unto you an Arabic Quran' (Q. 20:113). In this book all the quotations are from M. M. Pickthall's *The Meaning of the Glorious Koran* unless otherwise stated. However, I have not used his spelling '*Koran*' but rather '*Quran*' as being closer to the Arabic.

Comparison

It is incorrect to assume that the Quran is to the Muslim what the Bible is to the Christian. There is in the two faiths a different view of inspiration and revelation. In Islam the claim is that God has revealed his will in an eternal book, the Quran, while the Christian claim is that God has revealed himself in the eternal living word, Jesus Christ.

Muslims and Christians also have a different approach to the acquiring, handling and reading of their holy books. I became acutely aware of this when I was visiting the shrine of the patron saint of the Pakistani city of Lahore, Hazrat Data Ganj Bakhsh. In one of the stalls of the shrine complex I saw a bowl on which was inscribed in Arabic the Light verse from the Quran (Q. 24:35). I enquired about its price and was told that the *offering* for it was ten rupees. Never again did I seek to buy a copy of the Quran or anything which had Quranic verses written on it. I realised that, for the Muslim, the eternal word of the eternal God is so sacred that it is beyond price and cannot be purchased. One can only make a token gift. Later, in Ferozons Bookshop in Lahore, when acquiring a Quran in Arabic with Urdu and English parallel 'translations', I asked how much the offering was. My offering was accepted. Payment, in Muslim eyes, would have been dishonouring to Allah and disrespectful to what they so highly cherish – the 'glorious Quran'.

Recitation

Muslims take great care of Qurans, wrapping them up and keeping them on special stands. They never place them on the floor. The word Quran means 'recitation' and Muslims generally recite it aloud. The Quran has been divided into 30, 60 and 120 sections to make it easy for corporate as well as personal recitation. At a gathering where the Quran is recited aloud different readers will read different sections at the same time. Thus the whole book, which is about the size of the New Testament, can be easily read in one evening. Gatherings are single sex, more generally male. Everyone present will consider himself or herself blessed because the whole book has been read in their presence. Forgiveness is asked in case any word has been mispronounced. The eternal words whether understood or not confer blessing. This emphasis on recitation does not mean that the meaning is not important. The study of the Quran and its exposition is a central feature of Islamic studies and the foundation of the mosque teaching.

How to study the Quran

Someone unfamiliar with the Quran will find the usual order of the 114 surahs or chapters comprising 6,236 verses or *ayat* strange. Those surahs revealed to Muhammad in Mecca in 610–22 are distinguished by their headings from those revealed in Medina in 622–32. The order of surahs is not chronological. The first surah, the *Fatihah* or 'the opening', is often called 'the essence of the Quran' and consists of seven verses. After this the remaining 113 surahs are arranged in order of length, starting with the longest. It is thought that the first surah to be revealed to Muhammad was 96 which begins with the words:

> Read: In the name of the Lord who createth,
> Createth man from a clot.
> Read: And thy Lord is the Most Bounteous,
> Who teacheth by the pen . . . (*The Clot*, Q. 96:1–4)

After some months surah 74 was probably revealed.

> O thou wrapped up in thy raiment!
> Keep vigil . . .
> For We shall charge thee with a word of weight.
> (*The Enshrouded One*, Q. 74:1–2, 5)

Chapters and verses

Every surah in the Quran except for Surah 9 has the bismillah at the beginning, that is, 'In the name of Allah, the Beneficent, the Merciful'. The new reader needs to note that in the various translations or paraphrases there is a sometimes slight variation in verse numbering. Each surah has a name taken from the text of the particular surah. Sometimes this name denotes the main subject of the *surah*, for example, surah 19 is entitled *Mary* and is about the Virgin Mary and her son, Jesus. Other surahs may have titles which refer to a detail in the text, for example, surah 16 is entitled *The Bee* based on verse 68: 'And thy Lord inspired the bee, saying: Choose thou habitations in the hills and in the trees and in that which they thatch.'

Subject matter

The Quran is not a history book although historical events, especially those of the years of Muhammad's ministry, form its background. Neither is the Quran a book of theology. Rather it is a collection of warnings, exhortations, addresses, descriptive and narrative passages, allegorical sayings, prayers, liturgy and detailed laws and instructions. Reading the Quran straight through is probably not the best method for the initial approach. It would be better to read the first surah which Muslims recite in their prayers or *salat* five times a day. One might like to compare this prayer with the Lord's prayer recorded in the Bible (Matthew 6:9–13). After that one can select surah 96 called *The Clot*, as it was probably the first piece of the Quran to be revealed to Muhammad in the cave on Mount Hira near Mecca. Surah 112 named *The Daybreak* is another short surah and easy to understand.

Passages about Jesus

Of the longer passages about Jesus, Surah 19 called *Mary* is about the Virgin Mary and her son. The Quranic name for Jesus is Isa and the titles *ibn Maryam* (son of Mary) and *Al Masih* (the Messiah) are given to him. The birth and life of Mary, the annunciation (Q. 3:37–43), the birth of Isa, his mission, his miracles, his death and his relationship to God are all referred to in the Quran. The Quran confirms the previous scripture (Q. 2:91), the law or *tawrat* revealed to Moses (Q. 2:87), the psalms or *zabur* revealed to David (Q. 4:163) and the gospel or *injil* revealed to Jesus (Q. 5:46–8).

Law and Judgment

There are passages about creation, laws relating to marriage, theft, usury and obedience to parents. A summary of the moral law is given in surah 2:177:

> it is not righteousness that ye turn your faces to the East and the West; but righteous is he who believeth in Allah and the Last Day and the angels and the Scripture and the Prophets; and giveth his wealth, for love of Him, to kinsfolk and to orphans and the needy and the wayfarer and to those who ask, and to set slaves free; and observeth proper worship and payeth the poor-due . . .

There is frequent mention in the Quran about the Last Day and God's Judgment.

Cancelled verses and abrogation

The concept of abrogation has puzzled some critics as it seems strange that part of an eternal book could be replaced. However, sometimes what proved to be temporary instructions were given to the early Muslims and then superseded by later commands. Because of the eternity of the book both are found in the text and are to be recited (Q. 2:106): 'Such of Our revelations as We abrogate or cause to be forgotten, we bring (in place) one better or the like thereof. Knowest thou not that Allah is Able to do all things?'

Such a small book as the Quran is obviously not specific enough to give God's directions for every detail of daily life. So we must now turn to the Traditions of Islam which are nearly as important as the Quran itself. Generally, non-Muslims have underestimated the position of the traditions so let us now consider them.

The Sunnah and the Traditions

Definitions

The Sunnah and the Traditions are basically the same. The word Sunnah means the custom, habit and usage of the

Prophet. This includes his behaviour, how he did things, his sayings and declarations. These form a body of rules and examples to be followed in detail, for example, a man should trim his beard exactly as Muhammad trimmed his. Al-Ghazali refers to the pious man who wanted to eat a melon but did not dare to do so as he did not know the exact way in which Muhammad ate melon. The object of such detailed following of Muhammad's example is to develop the same piety and devotion as Muhammad displayed in all he did and said.

The Traditions or *Hadith* as they are called in Arabic are the collections of the words and actions of Muhammad, and sometimes those of his Companions. The word *hadith* means piece of information, account, narrative and record. Muhammad is regarded as the ideal man, the example, so it is very important to know exactly how he spoke and acted. 'Verily in the messenger of Allah ye have a good example for him who looketh unto Allah and the Last Day, and remembereth Allah much (Q. 33:21).

There are also Traditions called *Hadith Qudsi* (holy traditions) which are said to be words of Allah revealed to Muhammad but not recorded in the Quran. One well-known example of such a *hadith* is: 'Allah has said ask from me through mentioning My names.'

Reliability

Each tradition has a text called *matn* in Arabic and a chain of witnesses (*isnad*) through which the reliability of the text is supported. Both the text and the chain comprise the *hadith*. The chain of a *hadith* will be like this: F told me, saying E said D had informed him, saying C mentioned that he heard B relate, 'I heard A (a 'companion' of Muhammad) say to the Apostle of God . . .'. The *hadith* are generally grouped under subjects. There are hundreds of thousands of *hadith*. Those that were regarded as authentic were collected into six compilations during the ninth and early tenth centuries. There were other collections but these six formed the canonical *sunan* (Principles of Right Action): the *Sahih* (Genuine) of Al-Bukhari (d. 889), the *Jami* (Collection) of al-Tirmidhi (d. 892), al-Nasai (d. 915) and Ibn Maja al-Qazwini (d. 887).

An example

Al-Bukhari is said to have examined over 600,000 *hadith*, of which he judged only 4,000 to be genuine. An example is 'Uthman . . . said . . . I heard the Messenger of Allah, peace and blessings of Allah be on him, say: "Whoever builds a mosque, desiring Allah's pleasure, Allah builds for him the like of it in Paradise" ' (Bukhari 8:65).

Biographies of Muhammad

The key biography

The most famous and exhaustive Arabic biography of Muhammad and the closest to the sources is the *Sirat Rasul Allah* (Life of the Prophet of God) written by Ibn Ishaq (707–73) and edited by Ibn Hisham (d. 840). While it is not a sacred text, it is of extreme importance in view of who Muhammad was, and his position as 'the messenger of Allah and Seal of the Prophets' (Q. 33:40). Ibn Ishaq was born and bred in Medina where he started collecting stories and accounts about the life of Muhammad. On coming into conflict with two of the religious leaders in his city he moved to Egypt. Later he was invited to Baghdad where he died. Ibn Hisham edited Ibn Ishaq's collected works, incorporating them into this seminal biography on which almost all subsequent biographers have drawn.

Two battles

Muslims find it much easier than others who recite or read the Quran to see the relevance of particular passages to occurrences in Muhammad's life, partly because of their greater familiarity with the biographical material. As an example of this we can look at the third surah entitled *The Family of Imran*. Verses 13, 123 and 165 refer to Muhammad's victory at the battle of Badr, and verse 121 refers to his defeat the following year at the battle of Uhud. Verse 13 reads: 'There was a token for you in two hosts which met: one army fighting in the way of Allah, and another disbelieving, whom they saw as twice their number, clearly, with their very eyes. Thus

Allah strengthened with His succour whom He will. Lo! herein verily is a lesson for those who have eyes.' While verse 123 reads: 'Allah had already given you the victory at Badr, when ye were contemptible. So observe your duty to Allah in order that ye may be thankful.' The battle of Mount Uhud is referred to in two verses before: 'And remember when thou settest forth at daybreak from thy household to assign to the believers their position for the battle, Allah was Hearer, Knower.' Most of the third surah is about these two battles fought in the second and third years after the Hijrah or migration to Medina.

Jihad, or holy war

It is perhaps not surprising to find in this surah *Imran* teaching about jihad or holy war and the reward for those who are killed while engaged in it. This concept of jihad continues to stir Muslims to lay down their lives 'in the way of Allah' in Iraq, in Bosnia and in Afghanistan today. Verse 195 states:

> And their Lord heard them (and He saith): Lo! I suffer not the work of any worker, male or female, to be lost. Ye proceed from one another. So those who fled and were driven forth from their homes and suffered damage for My cause, and fought and were slain, verily I shall remit their evil deeds from them and verily I shall bring them into Gardens underneath which rivers flow – A reward from Allah. And with Allah is the fairest of rewards.

This military action is the 'lesser' or 'outer' jihad that has played a major role in Islamic history, at first defensive and later offensive, often because the Muslims felt threatened. We should note, however, that the Arabic root from which jihad comes means 'strive' with all one's might, 'struggle', 'fight', 'striving' in the way of Allah. The 'greater' or 'inner' jihad is an inward and more difficult struggle against one's passions. It also includes struggle for Islam in any area of life. For example, the former Tunisian President Bourguiba called the struggle against under-development a jihad.

Questions

For those who are not Muslims the Quran poses a number of questions, some of which have also been raised by Muslims. One example is that of the Mutazilites in the second Islamic century. They held a rationalist view: if God is one and eternal how can there be another eternal, that is the eternal Quran? If there are two eternals then there are two gods which is anathema to all Muslims. The Sunnis replied that God has seven eternal attributes, one of which is Word or Speaker. So the eternal God in his eternal capacity as Speaker speaks the eternal word which is the eternal Quran. The Mutazilites replied that this makes matters worse for if there are seven eternal attributes then we have not just two but eight gods. The Mutazilites concluded that the Quran was not an eternal book and so preserved their view of the unity of God. They hold a minority and very unacceptable view in the eyes of most Muslims. The concept of the eternal God and the eternal Quran helps some Muslims to understand the biblical view of the Trinity – three in one – three eternals but eternally one God.

We have already mentioned the question of the abrogation or the replacing of earlier injunctions by later ones and how the Muslims solved this problem for themselves, retaining both versions in their scripture. The question of why an eternal book seems to draw on sources from, for example, Judaism, Christianity and animism also puzzles many non-Muslims.

So far in Islam textual criticism is in its infancy. There is an unwillingness to submit the eternal text to the kind of study which is made of manuscripts of the Bible or the plays of Shakespeare. Queries of this sort need not hinder us from studying either the Quran or Hadith. It is always helpful to take a careful look at what so many people hold in such high honour. Let us conclude the chapter with a prayer that Muslims themselves use in approaching what to them is an eternal book. It is included in Constance Padwick's famous book *Muslim Devotions* and it helps us to see the depth of devotion and reverence for the Quran.

A prayer for Readers of the Quran from a prayerbook by Ali Muhammad al-Qari (the book was bought in Cairo):

*

Increase our longing for it [the Word of God in the Quran]; multiply our delight in it, to the number of raindrops and the leaves on the trees. Through it, perfect our confidence in the guidance of the good and the glad tidings of men of spiritual experience. Bring to our minds what we have forgotten of it. Teach us what we do not know of its radiant truths and secret touches of meaning. Make it for us an imam (normally a religious guide) and light and guidance and mercy in the abode below and the abode everlasting. And grant us the reading of it in the hours of night and the seasons of the day.

1. *The Qur'an translated, with a critical re-arrangement of the Surahs,* tr. Richard Bell (T. & T. Clark, 1930, repr. 1960), vol. II, p. 491.

5

Fundamental Doctrines

God

Sometimes people enquire if Muslims and Christians worship the same God. I have asked several Muslims who have become Christians if they worship the same God. All but one has replied that they worship the same God but now know him more personally in the Lord Jesus Christ. Another answer might be Yes and No – the subject is the same but the predicate is different. The understanding of God is different and therefore the description is in some measure different.

One might illustrate this with a diagram showing two over-lapping circles. The overlap is what is common (the subject), while the rest of the circles indicates differences (the predicate). Some question as to whether the subject is the same. Some Christians are mistakenly reluctant to use the name Allah. In Arabic it is the normal word for God so there is no real choice. Allah was used in Arabic Christian poetry before the rise of Islam. Allah = Al+Ilah = the deity. Both the Quran and the Bible declare that God is creator, that he is transcendent, that he is eternal and that he is merciful. In the descriptions of each shared attribute there is that which is found in both faiths, but also that which differs.

In the Quran Allah is the name of essence; the name for his essential being which is power. All other names are attributes only. In the earliest chapters or surahs of the Quran the omnipotence of God, that is the ability to do anything, is even more prominent than his unity. His essence is power which enables him to override his attributes and use them as he wills. 'Thus Allah sendeth astray whom He will, and whom He will He guideth . . .' (Q. 74:31).

Allah's leading attribute, mercy, is included in the bismillah, the phrase heading every chapter in the Quran except one. Of the traditional ninety-nine names twenty-six are not actually in the Quran but are based on Quranic passages near to them in meaning. The twenty-six are found in the Traditions. Love, a rare attribute in the Quran, is conveyed by the name *Wadud* which means affection – the affection with which the master responds to the loyalty of a faithful servant.

Sometimes one sees a Muslim reciting the names of God using a rosary divided into three sets of thirty-three beads. Among the group of names describing the self-subsistent unity of Allah, four are found in the following verse: 'He is the First and Last, and the Outward and the Inward . . .' (Q. 57:3). This is a favourite verse for the Sufis, the mystics of Islam. The four titles mentioned are known as 'the mothers of the attributes'. We are familiar with this Arabic expression for greatness, size and source ever since Saddam Hussein constantly used it for the 'mother of battles'.

Some main differences in the Quranic and biblical views of God

The doctrine of God is fundamental in both faiths and the differences in the respective concepts of God underlie some of the misconceptions that are prevalent.

1. God is not Father according to the Quran. It is daring for any Muslim to call God Father as Christians do in the Lord's prayer. In her autobiography the high-born Pakistani woman called Bilquis Sheikh recounts how a nun in Holy Family Hospital, Rawalpindi, Pakistan who saw the Bible on her bedside table said: 'Mrs Sheikh, why don't you pray to God as if he were your Father?' Later she describes how she did this and how she then was able to pour out her soul before God. God became someone with whom she had a living relationship. She deliberately entitled her book *I Dared to Call Him Father*. Islam denies that God shares any attribute with humanity.

2. According to Islam God's omnipotence means that he

can do whatever he wills. There is no harmony of his attributes, as by his essence, which is power, he can overrule everything. The Bible teaches that God cannot act contrary to his nature (Numbers 23:19). His attributes are in harmony with each other.

3. The name *Wadud* occurs twice in the Quran (Q. 11:92 and 85:14). This is the love of a master for a faithful servant, not of a father for his son. Allah only loves those who love him, which is in contrast to what the Apostle John writes in his first letter (1 John 4:16).

4. God is not absolutely, unchangeably just. He can change the ground rules. His law is not the expression of his moral nature but of his free will. The word 'holy' (Arabic *quddus*) is used only once in the Quran (Q. 59:23), where it indicates ceremonial not moral holiness. The word emphasises the 'otherness' of God. So even where there is agreement about an attribute, such as that God is holy, there will be disagreement about its meaning and the amount of weight to be given it.

Despite these distinctions we can note that Muslims call Jews and Christians 'the people of the book', recognising an affinity with them as they too seek to worship one God and creator, basing their beliefs on revelation and scripture.

Humanity

In five separate verses the Quran speaks of the purpose of God's creation of humankind. Only one verse declares the purpose to be the worship of God (Q. 51:56). The other four verses give the purpose as obedience or submission to God. The primary relationship between God and each individual is that of a master and servant or lord and slave. Abdullah, a very popular name, means the slave or servant of God. Each individual is created as a steward responsible for his or her actions and is God's vice-regent or *khalifah* on earth (Q. 6:166). Humankind is descended from one pair, Adam and Eve, and is originally of one community or *ummah* (Q. 10:20). All things are subjected to Adam (Q. 14:32–3), who is created to grow old (Q. 30:54), and before whom the angels prostrated themselves (Q. 38:72–5).

Sin

In discussing the subject of sin with my Muslim fellow-passenger on a boat in Bangladesh we both agreed that we are sinners. However, our perceptions and definitions were different. She meant that she was born innocent but spiritually weak with a bent towards evil (Q. 4:28) and that on growing out of babyhood she did sins and therefore became a sinner. I, on the other hand, meant that I was born a sinner being conceived in a state of sinfulness like all children of Adam. Soon I acted in ways which confirmed the condition in which I was born.

One word used five times for sin in the Quran means missing the mark or standard set by God. Two other words used dozens of times refer chiefly to ceremonial offences like not keeping the Ramadan fast or not praying regularly. The teaching of the Quran about sin is very sparse. In the Quran God's pronouncements relate to specific acts of sin, rather than defining sin generally as an offence against God's holiness. Only those acts are sin which Allah decrees should be regarded as such.

In summary the Quran teaches the following about sin:

1. The fall of Adam into sin was not a moral fall but only a mistake. Almost immediately God accepted Adam's repentance. He lost paradise but was not estranged from God (Q. 2:35–8).

2. The greatest sin is *shirk* or idolatry, the associating of anyone or anything with God (Q. 6:101–2).

3. Other sins are divided into big sins like breaking the ceremonial laws, theft, murder, adultery, gambling, drinking alcohol, eating pork, and usury. Breaking the ceremonial laws means failing to pray five times a day, failing to give alms or to keep the fast of Ramadan and not going on pilgrimage when it is possible.

4. Lying and anger are examples of little sins (Q. 5:90; 16:115 and 2:275–6).

5. Sin does not grieve God and he is unaffected by it. Sin harms the law-breaker (Q. 7:55).

Repentance

Surah 9 is called *Repentance*. The definition of repentance obviously depends on one's definition of sin. The general opinion of orthodox Muslim theologians is that repentance is not a permanent forsaking of evil but a turning after each act of sin. Repentance is turning from sin to Allah (Q. 24:31), and amendment of life (Q. 4:17). Humanity is called to repentance. Repentance is a work which contributes towards success and salvation. The Muslim does not generally repent because he has done something against God, but because he has done something against God's law. No atonement is necessary and each soul is responsible for its own actions. No soul can bear the burden of another (Q. 6:165). Non-Muslims repent when they accept Islam.

Salvation

The noun 'salvation' appears only once in the Quran (Q. 40:41) but the verb related to it occurs several times. In Islam salvation refers only to the future. In all these cases it means escaping from hell-fire and perhaps achieving paradise. Salvation is for men and women alike. Good deeds annul or cancel evil deeds. Repentance, faith and good deeds are conditions for salvation. The faith which is a condition of salvation is specifically belief in what was revealed to Muhammad. Nobody can be certain of salvation – this would be presumption. Muslims rely on one or more of the following six ways to achieve salvation.

1. Doing good works, including observing the five practices or pillars on which the faith of Islam rests (Q. 47:2).
2. On being a Muslim and hoping therefore to enter paradise through the will and mercy of God (Q. 2:105).
3. Doing good works, having faith and avoiding big sins (Q. 19:60).
4. Through martyrdom. Martyrs are promised instant paradise (Q. 3:195).

5. Through the intercession of saints.
6. By following the mystic way of Islam.

It should be noted that the Quranic view of salvation is different from the biblical. It deals only with the future. Muslims and Christians are asking different questions. Christians are asking: 'How can I, in my sinful state, know the holy God and be reconciled to him?' Muslims are asking: 'How can I know God's laws so that I can follow them and be acceptable to him?'

A basic Muslim theology would centre round three major themes – God, prophethood and the last things (resurrection, judgment, heaven and hell). Prophethood is discussed in Chapter 8.

Muslim theologians often emphasise that God is one and that he has ninety-nine names and seven eternal attributes – seeing, hearing, life, purpose, will, speech, and knowing. There are six articles of faith and five pillars on which the faith rests.

Muslims list the six articles of faith or *iman* as belief in (1) God; (2) God's angels – including Gabriel and three other archangels; (3) God's books – including books revealed to Adam, Seth, Enoch and Abraham which have been lost; and the Pentateuch, the Psalms, the Gospel and the Quran; (4) God's apostles, of whom the six greatest are Adam, Noah, Abraham, Moses, Isa (Jesus) and Muhammad; (5) God's judgment; (6) God's decrees 'for good and evil, sweet and bitter'. The five pillars are set out in the next chapter.

Eschatology or the Last Things

Natural calamities like earthquakes and tornadoes are considered by Muslims as possible preludes to end of the world and the winding up of human history. Descriptions of heaven and hell, of the day of resurrection and judgment are very vivid in Muslim writings. In his famous book on ethics the theologian Al-Ghazali has a section on 'Death and What Follows'. It includes the following subjects: the agony of death;

the decease of Muhammad, and of several of the caliphs; dying words of caliphs and saints and sayings of Sufi saints about biers and graveyards; what the dead encounters in the grave until the trumpet blast announcing the resurrection; what is known of the states of the dead from the trumpet blast until settling in paradise or in the fire; a description of the trumpet blast; the length of the day of resurrection; the questioning; the balance; the antagonist; the bridge; the intercession; and a final description of hell and of paradise.[1]

1. Summarised from D. M. Donaldson, *Studies in Muslim Ethics* (SPCK, 1963), p. 165.

6

Spirituality and Worship

Piety and devotion are part of everyday Muslim life. When living in a Muslim environment one is always aware of the daily ritual. The dawn call to prayer before the noise of the city has properly started will linger as a memory with anyone who has lived in a Muslim land. It is chanted in Arabic by the muezzin (the one who gives the *azzan* or call to prayer). Sometimes the call to prayer is prerecorded and then broadcast through loudspeakers. The text varies a little according to the rite or school of Islamic law prevalent in the area. Here is one translation of the call to prayer:

God is most great (*Allahu Akbar)*, (four times)
I testify there is no god but God (twice)
I testify that Muhammad is the Messenger of God (twice)
Come to prayer (twice)
Come to success (twice)
God is most great (once)
There is no god but God (once)
Prayer is better than sleep (at dawn only).

Ritual prayer is called *salat* and is the second of the five pillars described below.

The Five Pillars

1. *Witness or* shahadah
The first pillar is the recitation of the creed or witness: 'I bear

witness that there is no god but God and Muhammad is the
Messenger of God.' This is fundamental and its recitation in
Arabic twice in front of two witnesses can make a person a
Muslim. The Kingdom of Saudi Arabia has this witness on
its national flag.

2. *Ritual prayer or* salat

From puberty on, after the prescribed ablutions, all Muslims
are required to offer the five daily prayers. Ritual prayers can
be said in private or in a mosque or special prayer area. Women
generally say their prayers in the privacy of their home or in
the place in the mosque designated for them. However, not
many mosques have such places. Most mosques have a clock
and list the times for prayer which vary as the days shorten
or lengthen. The prescribed five times are: dawn prayer before
sunrise, noon prayer, afternoon prayer, evening prayer just
after sunset, and night prayer.

First the Muslim stands facing the *Kaaba* in Mecca with
open hands and palms forward at head height and recites
the first *Allahu Akbar.* Then with hands by his side he recites
the first chapter or surah of the Quran which is called the
Fatihah (literally 'opening'). It is usual for him while still
standing to recite one or two verses of the Quran, making
his own choice. After that he expresses his adoration of God
by making a deep bow from the chest, standing upright
again and then prostrating himself with knees and forehead
to the ground. He then sits back on his heels and again
prostrates himself with his head to the ground. Towards
the end of the prayer while on his knees he silently recites the
declaration of faith and at other times of silence he may
make his individual petitions, especially for forgiveness.
After the last *raka* he, still on his knees, offers salutations of
peace to the right and left to those next to him, or if he is
alone to his two guardian angels. This Arabic word *raka*
literally means a 'bowing', and is used to describe one cycle
of six movements or positions in daily ritual prayer as well
as the second position in particular. There are generally two
rakas at dawn prayers, three at sunset and four at the other
times.

The first surah is recited as part of the daily ritual prayer all over the world.

> Praise be to Allah, Lord of the Worlds,
> The Beneficent, the Merciful.
> Owner of the Day of Judgment,
> Thee (alone) we worship: Thee (alone) we ask for help.
> Show us the straight path,
> The path of those whom Thou hast favoured:
> Not (the path) of those who earn Thine anger nor of those
> who go astray.

Communal prayer on Fridays follows the same ritual except that there is a long sermon between the second and the third *rakas*.

Prayer brings people nearer to God. 'And when my servants question thee concerning Me, then surely I am nigh. I answer the prayer of the suppliant when he crieth unto Me. So let them hear My call and let them trust in Me, in order that they may be led aright' (Q. 2:186).

These regular prayers are a spiritual, moral and physical discipline, strengthening obedience to God.

3. *Welfare contribution or* zakat
Zakat is an obligatory payment of 2.5 per cent of a Muslim's income towards helping the poor and social projects. The root of the Arabic word *zakat* signifies purification. *Zakat* is regarded as an act of worship and contributes to a just society in which everyone can share. Certainly although there is much poverty and undernourishment it is unusual to find any Muslim starving in, for example, Muslim areas of the Indian subcontinent.

4. *The obligatory fast or* sawm
The Muslim fasts from dawn to sunset every day during the special month of Ramadan by refraining from eating, drinking, smoking and sexual intercourse. Children, the sick, travellers, pregnant women and nursing mothers and the aged are exempt from fasting. To many devout Muslims the fast of Ramadan

is an opportunity to exercise greater self-discipline, to perfect obedience to God, to give thanks for the revelation of the Quran first revealed during this month and to be reminded again of God's nearness and of the reality of the one community. It also increases awareness of the needs of the poor and of one's own need of spiritual as well as physical purification. The meals eaten at night are often celebrations, sometimes lavish, and add to the sense of communal unity.

5. *The pilgrimage or* hajj
Every Muslim is required to make this pilgrimage to the House of Allah (*Al-Kaaba*) in Mecca, Saudi Arabia, in the twelfth month of the Muslim calendar, at least once in their lifetime if it can be afforded. Sometimes the extended family club together to send two or three members as their representatives if they cannot all afford to go. Muslims come from all parts of the world and take part as equals in the pilgrimage, all wearing white ritual clothing. For many Muslims the pilgrimage is a powerful spiritual experience and a great penitential act through which remission of all past sins is obtained.

Pilgrims recite the following invocation in Arabic thousands of times during the first days of the pilgrimage and before going to a small hill called Mount Arafat. It is known in Arabic as *Jabal Ar-Rahman*, the Mount of Mercy, as Adam and Eve are said to have turned back to God in that place and then been forgiven and reunited with each other. The plain of Arafat is 24 km east of Mecca.

> You call us, we are here, O God! We are here!
> We are here, there is none beside You. We are here!
> Praise and good deeds belong to you, and the empire!
> There is none but You!

Other Aspects of Islamic Spiritual Life

Personal, informal prayer or dua
It is important to distinguish between ritual prayer or *salat*, and *dua* or informal, personal prayer. *Dua* consists of invoca-

tions, requests, intercessions, memorised and extempore prayer.
The literal meaning of *dua* is a cry or call. Many of these
prayers are written down in prayer manuals and books of
devotions. At bus stations and at railway bookshops the
traveller can buy little devotional books containing such
prayers. Individuals will also supplement these with their own
personal prayers in their own words and language. One of
my Muslim friends, telling me of her family problems, said:
'If it were not for prayer I do not know how I could have
coped.'

The Muslim religious calendar

The daily and weekly liturgical prayers are part of the
framework of the lunar calendar with its other festivals and
celebrations. The new moon marks the first day of each month
(Q. 10:6). The Islamic calendar begins with the *Hijrah*, the
day Muhammad 'emigrated' from Mecca to Medina to set
up his new social and political order. Muslims date everything
from that event which is usually considered to be 20 September
622 in the Gregorian calendar.

Since the average interval between new moons is twenty-
nine days, twelve hours, forty-four minutes and three seconds,
the lunar months alternate between twenty-nine and thirty
days in length. Any given month will have twenty-nine days
in some years and thirty days in others. The new moon must
also be visually sighted for the new month to start. Mathe-
matical calculation is not valid, so one can never be sure in
advance precisely when, for example, the month of *Ramadan*
will begin and one should start fasting.

It follows that, although the Islamic lunar year has twelve
months, it has only 354 days on an average. The Quran (9:36–
7) forbids the periodic insertion of a thirteenth month to keep
it in line with the solar year. So the Islamic calendar goes
backwards through the solar calendar about eleven days a
year, returning to the same solar time in about thirty-two solar
years.[1] We should note that Muslims, like Jews, reckon the
'day' (twenty-four hour period) begins in the evening. Therefore the 'night of the 27th of Ramadan' begins just after
sundown on the 26th. After Ramadan, the month of fasting,

on the first of the following month of Shawwal, the first of the required feasts, *Id al-fitr*, is celebrated to mark the end of the fast. People celebrate and wear new clothes. About sixty-nine days later comes the 'Feast of Sacrifice' called *Id al-adha*, the greater feast that commemorates Abraham's offering of his son, when each family generally sacrifices a sheep or goat or cow or camel. This Muslim festival is comparable in its importance to the greatest Christian festival – Easter.

Sufism

The personal and less formal side of Islam is shown in Islamic mysticism which is known as Sufism. The Sufis are the mystics of Islam. They are found among Sunnis as well as Shias who seek union with God through the mystic path. They often follow a spiritual guide, either individually or in small groups. There are also larger groups called brotherhoods. Baha al-Din Naqshbandi (d. 791) founded Sufi groups in Iran and Bukhara. They practised the recollection of God in the act of inhaling and exhaling of breath.

> Music, banned from the mosque, came into its own in mystical devotions. Dervish dances probably had their roots in pre-Islamic ecstatic dances, but as organised by the Persian Rumi the 'whirling dervishes' gyrate round their sheikh in a representation of the planets circling the sun . . . reciting inwardly the name of God: Al-lah, Al-lah, Al-lah. With closed eyes they whirl, to the music of flutes, drums and strings, seeking union with the divine, till they cease and return to stillness.[2]

The disciple lights his lamp from the master's flame. First through initiation and then through discipline and devotion the followers seek a nearness with God that perhaps has eluded them in the worship in the mosque. They do not reject the outer law (Shariah) but seek more the inner reality. Some fundamentalist Muslims condemn the Sufis, especially when they seem to put more stress on the mystic path than on the ritual prayers. Sufism, however, is rooted in the Quran: 'We (Allah) are nearer to him (man) than his jugular vein' (Q. 50:16) and 'Men whom neither merchandise nor sale beguileth from remembrance of Allah' (Q. 24:37). Sufism is also rooted in the traditions or *hadith*: 'My Heaven cannot contain Me, nor can My earth, but the heart of My believing slave can contain Me' (*Hadith Qudsi*).

One of the greatest Sufis, Rabia al-Adawiya (d. 801) wrote:

My Lord, eyes are at rest, the stars are setting, hushed are the movements of the birds, of the monsters in the deep. And Thou art the Just who knoweth no change, the Equity that swerveth not, the Everlasting that passeth not away. The doors of kings are locked and guarded by their henchmen. But Thy door is open to whoso calleth on Thee. My Lord, each lover is now alone with his beloved. And I am alone with Thee.

I well remember a chorus sung with deep personal devotion by a Sufi neighbour as he walked along the street and suddenly turned the corner to where I was walking. Through the previous night his fraternity had been chanting and repeating the name of Allah as they often did. One special day in honour of their saint they processed through the village, over and over again repeating *Allahu, Allahu, Allahu*. They were remembering God by calling on his name.

Muhammad Veneration

Muhammad veneration goes right back to the beginning of historical Islam. Surah *Light* (Q. 24:35) describes God as the Light or *nur* and Muhammad as the Lamp which contains the Light. In Q. 32:24 Muhammad is described as a 'beautiful model' for believers. A *Hadith Qudsi* declares about Muhammad: 'If it had not been for you I would not have created the heavens.' There are 201 names for Muhammad. Many are the same as the names for God but without the definite article 'the': *Nur*, 'light,' as compared with *al-nur*, 'the light'. Light is often identified with God's absoluteness.

In the last twenty years or so there has been a revival of Muhammad veneration. Whereas before, the Prophet's birthday was celebrated quietly, now there are processions in many towns and villages. A few years ago there was a picture in *The Times* of a procession of about 5,000 Muslims leaving Hyde Park Corner in London. The newspaper commented that the Prophet's birthday was the only occasion or event which could unite all parties, sects and groupings among the million or so Muslims of the UK. Muslims are looking for new foci of unity to replace that supplied until 1924 by the Caliphate. Love and veneration for the Prophet are probably the strongest focus of unity. Muhammad Iqbal, the poet philosopher of the Indian subcontinent, wrote in one of his Persian poems translated by Professor A. J. Arberry: 'All our glory is for the name of Muhammad.'

A *qasida* is a poem in praise of a famous person – very often Muhammad. No other Arabic poem is as well-known as the *Qasida Burda* (The Prophet's Mantle). It has been translated into practically every language that Muslims use and more than ninety commentaries have been written on it especially in Arabic, Persian, Turkish and Berber. The poet, Muhammad ibn Said al-Busiri, from the town of Busir, lived in the thirteenth century AD. In despair, being paralysed by an incurable illness, he composed a poem praising Muhammad. Then he had a dream in which the Prophet came, massaged him and then wrapped him in his mantle or *burda*. He was cured! The poem became extremely popular and is recited all over the world by Muslims on special occasions. It is also used as an amulet. It appeals to non-Arabic speakers in that it gives a summary of the Prophet's life and of Muslim doctrine. Here are verses 34, 42 and 58 respectively from this famous poem from a translation made by James Ritchie.[3]

Muhammad, Lord of both worlds and both races
and both peoples, Arab and non-Arab.

He is free from peer in his excellent qualities
so that the essence of goodness is in him undivided.

No perfume (ointment) equals the earth which holds his
bones,
Blessed is he who smells it and kisses it.

Present-day Muhammad veneration is found in many forms.
In the front of the inside of most buses in Pakistan one reads
'Ya Allah' on one side and 'Ya Muhammad' on the other.
The invocation 'Ya' or (O) is only used for a living person
and so Wahhabis and strict fundamentalists will denounce
the honouring of a dead person in this way. The media in
Pakistan also pays attention to the cult of Muhammad
veneration, often calling him Saviour of the world and Lord
of the universe. A poem by Maulana Zafar Ali Khan taught
in the schools in Pakistan includes these lines:

Though my link with the divinity of God be severed,
May my hand never let go of the hem of the Chosen one.

The 'Chosen one' is Muhammad.

The Turkish *mevlud-sherif* by Suleyman Chelebi of Bursa
written about 1410 is also very famous. As Muhammad is
said to have died on his birthday it is sung not only on the
Prophet's birthday but on memorial days of a death as well. The
most famous part of it is the *Marhaba* (Welcome) which
creation sings when the light of Muhammad begins to radiate
on the night he was born. Here are a few lines:

Welcome, O high prince, we greet you! . . .
Welcome, O one who is not separated from God . . .
Welcome, O intercessor for the sinner!
Welcome, O prince of this world and the next!
Only for you Time and Space was created.

Clearly many Muslims feel the need of a mediator. So much
of what Christians say of Jesus they identify with Muhammad.
The great exception is the biblical emphasis on the sufferings
of Jesus. Whatever is said of Jesus's glory and majesty might
be transferred in the mind of the hearer but what is said of
his sufferings will not be appropriated, as to the Muslim they

are a sign of shame and defeat. That Jesus is 'now crowned with glory and honour because he suffered of death' (Hebrews 2:9) is still a Christian mystery.

Folk or Popular Islam

The Jewish, Christian and Muslim religions all lay claim to revelation. However, each reverts at different points and in varying degrees from what was revealed in scripture as the ideal to what might be called natural religion or even animism. In the Old Testament we find the Prophet Jeremiah rebuking his seventh-century fellow-townsmen because they regard the presence of the Temple in their city of Jerusalem as an automatic insurance policy against their enemies. It did not occur to them that their spiritual backsliding could bring them under the judgment of their righteous God and that he might use their enemies as his instrument of judgment (Jeremiah 7:1–8).

Many Muslims also fall into this trap of trying to manipulate and control God rather than be controlled by him. Sometimes, however, they are not so much trying to manipulate God as to contain Satan and evil jinn. The Quran states: 'I created the jinn and humankind only that they might worship me' (Q. 51:56). Some jinn have behaved in a malevolent way while others remained good influences. The respected Pakistani theologian Maulana Kausar Niazi wrote:

That the Jinns enter the body of human beings, take possession of them . . . is so positively true that, apart from arguments, it is upheld by experience also. The writings of innumerable doctors of theology are full of narrations how they, with the aid of the Divine word, made the Jinns flee from the bodies of the possessed. Even in these days a very pious scholar told the present writer that his wife had been ailing for many years. She underwent spasms. No amount of treatment could cure her. At last a person well versed in occult sciences was consulted. He told him that her ailment was a Jinn's mischief. Afterwards whenever she fell into a spasm, he recited the Quran. Slowly she began to recover and was finally delivered from the affliction. During moments of convulsion, the Jinn often talked to the pious man. He knew *Qasida Burda* by heart and could recite it nonstop, though the woman knew little about the *Qasida*. Once he asked the Jinn to give a proof of his existence. Suddenly a fresh and fragrant cardamom bough fell into his lap.[4]

Amulets containing verses of the Quran are worn round the neck as a form of protection in warding off evil. Many times I have asked Muslim women whether they think God prefers his word to be hanging round their necks or lodged in their hearts. Always they will say that God prefers his word to be in our hearts. As an extra insurance they continue to wear amulets in the same way as many secularly minded people wear lucky charms. Each group of verses in the *Qasida Burda* mentioned above is used as an amulet for particular purposes. Al-Bajuri, a famous commentator on the poem, says of verses 105–15 that if a man has a quarrel with a friend, and writes these verses on a lion's skin and puts it in the fold of his turban and then enters his friend's presence in silence his friend will open the conversation in a friendly fashion.[5]

The ninety-nine names of God are also often used as magical incantations. For example, about the name Al-Halim (which means The Forbearing One), it is said that no blight or harm will affect a farmer's crop if he writes this name *Ya-Halim* (which means O Forbearing One) as a prayer on a piece of paper and puts it with the seed he has sown. Fear of the evil eye and elaborate precautions against satanic influences are further evidences of this type of popular religion. Murray T. Titus in a chapter on saint-veneration wrote about the widespread belief in the powers of saints to heal and perform miracles.[6]

The graves of saints are visited by litigants seeking victory in law cases; by the farmer who lost a horse; by the woman who desires a child; by the father who seeks healing for his sick boy; by the merchant who desires prosperity in business; by the hunter who wants a lucky day; by the gambler, and even by the thief.

It would seem that not much has changed. Saints and shrines are still considered sources of advice and counsel on a wide range of matters. Dr Bill Musk[7] tells how some Muslims return from the UK to Pakistan or India or Bangladesh to consult the family holy man or *pir* for advice and help. To make such help more accessible some holy men or *pirs* have settled in the UK and shrines have been built in strongly Muslim areas. The Wahhabi reformers of Arabia, fundamentalist groups like the Muslim Brotherhood in the Arab world and the Jamaat-i-Islami in the Indian subcontinent, and those greatly influenced by secularism strongly condemn folk Islam and the excessive veneration of saints. Visiting the shrines of the saints or *marabouts* is forbidden in North Africa but people still flock to the shrines. Gradually the proper respect for Sufi martyrs and saints has declined into this kind of folk religion.

It should be noted, however, that astrology is countenanced in the Quran: 'Nay, I swear by the places of the stars' (Q. 56:75). It is common for ordinary Muslims to seek insight or guidance from the stars.

Underlying the revealed religions is a layer of animism which was there before the revelations came. Animism was extensively prevalent in pre-Islamic Arabia and we find traces of it in the orthodox beliefs and practices of Islam. The kissing of the black stone at the Kaaba in Mecca during the pilgrimage is another indication of animistic underlay. The Arabic word *kaaba* means 'cube' and is the name for the 15 metres high cube-shaped stone building said to have been built by the first man Adam and then rebuilt by the Prophet Abraham and his son Ishmael. Dedicated to the one God it had gradually been corrupted by Baal worship. During Muhammad's time it housed 360 deities. When he returned in triumph to Mecca from Medina he performed the ritual circumambulation seven times and then entered the shrine and destroyed all the idols. After this only Muslims could enter the Kaaba and indeed Mecca itself. The circling of the Kaaba seven times is one of the required acts of the Muslim pilgrimage in Mecca.

When one reflects on the strictly orthodox people of the mosque one cannot but be impressed by the devotion and discipline of the faithful. When one considers the multitudes who practise Islam in a more popular form and could be called the people of the shrine one is aware of the longing of the human heart for healing, deliverance, blessing and protection. Sufism and the brotherhoods with their emphasis on love for God and on his nearness fulfil a need for a sense of fellowship with God. Muhammad veneration also meets some of the need for nearness and mediation. After forty years in Asia and the Middle East I increasingly find that the discipline, devotion and piety of many Muslims commands respect.

1. I am indebted to Mr Samuel Schlorff for some of this information.
2. Geoffrey Parrinder, *Mysticism in the World's Religions* (Sheldon Press, 1976), pp. 130–1.
3. *Encounter*, nos. 171–2, Jan.–Feb. 1991.
4. *Creation of Man* (Sh. Muhammad Ashraf, 1975), pp. 48–9.
5. See Ritchie, *Encounter*, nos. 171–2, p. 18.
6. *Islam in India and Pakistan* (The Christian Society, Madras, 1959), p. 138.
7. *The Unseen Face of Islam* (MARC, 1989).

7

Ethics and Morality

Muhammad's Ethical Heritage

Generosity and hospitality were Arab virtues in pre-Islamic Arabia. Muhammad grew up in a tribal society in which relationships were both valuable and important. He experienced from his cradle the care and nurture of his extended family. He had lost both parents before he was seven. He was proud of belonging to his tribe, the Quraish, and to the wider community of Mecca. His environment must have influenced his view of basic moral virtues and vices, although he was certainly a reformer and did not accept all the views of his countrymen. He claimed to be God's Prophet on whom the Quran descended and that its teaching on morality and ethics came directly from God.

Quranic Teaching on Ethics

All ethical teaching in Islam has to be based on the authoritative Quran in which Allah has revealed his will. Such teaching is exemplified in the conduct or confirmed by the approval of the Prophet Muhammad and also confirmed by human reason and experience. The Quran stresses duty to Allah and one's fellow believers. It includes exhortations to humility, honesty, giving to the poor, kindness, moderation, forgiveness, and trustworthiness, while condemning vices such as boasting, blasphemy and slander. There are detailed injunctions about retaliation, oaths, rewards and punishments (Q. 5:38).

Regulations for the Muslim community include the care of orphans, divorce proceedings, debts and inheritances.

Predestination and free will and their relationship to morality became an issue early in Islamic history. There has been more discussion about human responsibility for actions in the light of God's sovereign decrees than about any other theological matter. Many Muslims as well as many outside Islam have difficulty condoning such practices as slavery, concubinage, polygamy, the enforced segregation of women and actual warfare in the name of religion. They are also puzzled by the idea that predestination to acceptance or rejection by God can be divorced from any consideration of justice or ethics. This involves the Quranic view of the nature of God. His greatness must not be thought of as being modified or limited by the perfection of any strictly moral qualities. Restriction on his freedom would limit his greatness. Similarly his will is not to be thought of as being limited in its operations to the sphere of ethics. As a consequence Allah sometimes seems both arbitrary and changeable in dealing with mankind (Q. 74:31).

In the Quran Abraham, Joseph, Moses, David and Solomon were repentant men of God, who sought God's assistance to do righteousness. Particularly at the time of the revelation of the early surahs Muhammad was in close touch with Jews and their teaching and urged his followers: 'question those who read the Scripture (that was) before thee . . .' (Q. 10:95). Little importance is given in the Quran to the moral teaching of Jesus and there is no reference to his parables.

Ethics in the Traditions and Muhammad as the 'Ideal Man'

The influence of the Traditions on Muslims is almost as great as that of the Quran, and in regard to ethics it is probably greater. The pious Muslim seeks to know God's will for every detail of life. Such a relatively small book as the Quran obviously cannot meet this need so the hundreds of thousands of 'sound' traditions furnish guidance for almost every situation in life. The Traditions together with the Quran are also main sources for building the profile of the Prophet Muhammad who is regarded as the 'ideal man', the pattern, to be copied in every detail. From the Traditions an account of Muhammad's actions, utterances and unspoken approval can be drawn. In ethics, as in religion, the ultimate ideal is submission to the will of God. This imitating of Muhammad as the exemplar, displaying the ideal standard for conduct, establishes Muslim ethics as different from Christianity. Christians, while committed to imitating the example of Christ, are taught in the Bible that this is not enough. The Quran teaches that God will not change the condition of a people until they first change what is in their hearts (Q. 13:11), but the Bible requires radical individual transformation by the power of the Holy Spirit. Imitation is inadequate to bring this about but it helps in seeing the necessity of it.

Whatever in the Quran and Traditions relates to ceremonial duties, legal practices and theological beliefs is called Sunnah. Whatever throws light on how Muhammad lived and taught is called *Sira*; while the third grouping of the material relates to the requirements for good manners, education and culture, and is called *Adab*. Muhammad must have had an attractive and charismatic personality. In the *Sira* his kindliness, amiability and friendliness are noted, together with his accessibility. In a well-known Tradition Muhammad said: 'Falsehood is permitted only on three occasions – war, which is itself deceit, or when a man brings about a reconciliation between two persons, or when a man seeks to please his woman.' It is interesting that in Islamic literature the great majority of proverbs are attributed either to Muhammad himself, or to one or other of his Companions, or, in the case of the Shias, to one of their imams.

Al-Ghazali's Ethical Teachings

The ethics of Islam include the valuable contributions made by ascetics; and the individual struggles of Muslim mystics (Sufis) to master their inner life in relation to the will of their creator. Al-Ghazali was one of these. This famous theologian, philosopher and mystic was mentioned in Chapter 2. He was regarded as the Renewer of Islam's sixth century and was called 'The Proof of Islam'. His most famous book is the Arabic *Ihya al-Ulum al-Din* (The Quickening of Religious Knowledge). Book 1 has a section entitled 'On The Marvels of the Heart'. It describes how the servant of God is strongly tempted by imaginings, notions, and projects; and how he should invoke the name of God against temptations. Change of heart is also discussed. Book 2 includes a treatise called 'On the Duties of Brotherhood' which deals with material and personal aid, holding one's tongue and speaking out as appropriate. In the section on forgiveness Al-Ghazali mentions how tenderness and comfort can inspire repentance. Other brotherly duties dealt with include intercessory prayer as well as loyalty, sincerity and informality.

Ethics of the Persian Sufi Poets

Jalal al-Din al-Rumi (1207–73) lived for forty years as a Sufi lecturer and poet at Qoniya in Turkey, and was founder of the order of Mawlawis, best known as dancing dervishes. In his account of Sufism Rumi tends to abolish the distinction between good and evil – the latter becoming an aspect of not-being with no real existence. Human personality is, therefore, a transient phenomenon which ultimately disappears in what alone is real – the eternal being of God.

Shaik Muslih al-Din Saadi, (1184–circ.1292) was the most popular of all the Persian poets. His chief work the *Gulistan*, (The Rose Garden), although an ethical treatise, follows no particular ethical theory. Saadi was a moralist rather than a mystic. Many of his sayings relate to the daily contact of ordinary men with one another. For example: 'Do not destroy your brother's reputation in a single street, lest fortune destroy your fair name throughout the whole city.'

Modern Ethical Interpretations of Islam

Jamal al-Din al-Afghani (d. 1897) regarded Islam as a world religion thoroughly capable, through its inner spirituality, of adapting to the varying conditions of every age. Another influential reformer was the Egyptian, Muhammad Abduh (d. 1905). He encouraged assimilation of Western civilisation, without abandoning fundamental Muslim ideas. The best known of the modern Indian ethical interpreters of Islam is Dr Muhammad Iqbal. In his *Reconstruction of Religious Thought in Islam* he discussed human immortality, interpreting the Quran to his own satisfaction as a philosopher. Iqbal believed that *taqdir* or predestination does not mean that the actions of each individual have been determined by God beforehand. He was an evolutionary thinker, propounding that not only human beings but the whole universe is rising from a lower to a higher level according to God's purpose.

The usual Muslim idea of virtue is doing good to humankind, in obedience to the will of God, and for the sake of everlasting happiness. The defects of an ethical system based on a doctrine of rewards and punishments is that it reduces conduct to selfish prudence and lacks the love of goodness for its own sake.

Ecology

Those who wish to study how five major religions treat the question of ecology might wish to look at the series of books produced on *World Religions and Ecology*. I am indebted to one in the series, *Islam and Ecology*,[1] for stimulating my thinking on this subject. I was first made aware of the importance that the Quran and contemporary Muslims placed on this when the Sultanate of Oman hosted an international conference to address the subject of how nations might cooperate in the stewardship of world resources. As far as I know the above-mentioned is the first book to make a comprehensive presentation of the Islamic position on ecology – indeed its preface makes this claim.

About five hundred verses in the Quran and many traditions deal with the environment and how man is to treat it. An early Muslim legal scholar, Abu al-Faraj, said: 'People do not in fact own things, for the real owner is their Creator; they only enjoy the usufruct of things, subject to the Divine Law.' The Quran repeatedly urges us to maintain the balance of nature and not to upset it (Q. 30:41). The Quran lays emphasis on God's role as creator and sustainer and regards humans as God's stewards and regents on earth, with the duty of looking after the earth in their care. Islam acknowledges that humans are not the only creatures that are worthy of protection and cherishing. 'There is not an animal in the earth, nor a flying creature flying on two wings, but they are peoples like unto you. We have neglected nothing in the Book (of Our decrees). Then unto their Lord they will be gathered' (Q. 6:38).

Islam and Christianity come close together in their acknowledgment of God as creator and so find some common ground in ecological and environmental issues. The secular humanist would also join in this concern but from a different perspective and for different reasons. Three world-views happen to coincide on this issue.

Population, Birth-Control and Abortion

Muslim governments continue to introduce reforms which they claim are not repugnant to the Quran and the Sunnah. As overpopulation is a major problem for many Muslim lands the question of family planning is crucial. Many governments give positive support to family planning programmes and contraceptive services. A Turkish family planning poster reads as follows (in translation): 'Family planning does not mean prevention of births! The Holy Quran says "Have as many children as you can look after." ' A Pakistani Family Planning Association poster produced in Urdu and Arabic for World Population Year says: 'Emphatically too many children bring poverty (Abdullah Ben Abbas).' Abdullah Ben Abbas was an intimate of Muhammad with the reputation of being the greatest authority in exegesis of the Quran at that time.

Despite organised government efforts in many countries Muslim lands still have the highest percentage of population increase a year, generally around 2.9 per cent. Ignorance and fear make some slow to adopt family planning techniques. Sometimes one spouse is willing and the other is not. Religious advisers – saints at their shrines – are often against such devices which would reduce the number of Muslims.

Reinforcing these hindrances to family planning is the great fear of Muslim parents that they will not have enough sons. How often a wife is in distress because she has not produced a child. The wife who produces only daughters will seek religious and perhaps medical help. If she has one son she will want more sons in case the son dies, as he may so easily do. Some Muslims argue that abortion differs from contraception in that it is an assault on life and so can be called a criminal act. The foetus has the right to live but danger to the mother's life or the strong possibility of a deformed baby are grounds on which abortion could be allowed. Whatever the teaching about abortion and the advice of medical, religious or government leaders there is a tremendous demand for legal and illegal abortion. Illegal abortion is widely practised and much harm is done to women and children through medically questionable methods. Pressures of poverty and social morality (in the case of illegitimate pregnancies) drive many women to take desperate measures and there are always those who exploit them for financial gain.

Most governments permit abortions on medical grounds. Tunisia allows abortion on social grounds also. It is interesting that in Ayatollah Khomeini's Iran the laws legalising voluntary sterilisation and abortion on both medical and social grounds were repealed. At first, the Islamic Revolutionary Government closed all family planning clinics and contraceptives were removed from all pharmacies. However, after pressure from women, the Ministry of Health issued a statement about conditions under which birth control is permissible. At the UN Conference on Population and Development held in Cairo in September 1994 the Roman Catholic and Muslim representatives found they were allies in their strict views about birth control. Dr Abdel Rahim Omran,[2] in his book *Family Planning in the Legacy of Islam* (1992), concludes that birth-control is authorised in Islam but that it is hindered by lack of health education and by poverty.

Women in Islam

One of the most charming books that I have read in recent years is *The Harem Within: Tales of a Moroccan Girlhood* by Fatima Mernissi.[3] *The Sunday Times* commented on her book: 'The women of Islam have been speaking out for fourteen centuries, but none has been more eloquent that Fatima Mernissi. A leading Muslim feminist and sociologist, she combines intellect with scholarship . . .' In another of her books she shows how Muhammad, far from being an oppressor of women, upheld the spiritual equality of all in Islam.[4] Undoubtedly, this is the position of the Quran: 'Whosoever doeth right, whether male or female, and is a believer, him verily We shall quicken with good life, and We shall pay them a recompense in proportion to the best of what they used to do' (Q. 16:97). The Quran also teaches that men and women have different but complementary roles in society, in that they have different functions and responsibilities. The traditions of Islam sometimes give another picture. Mernissi asked her grocer if a woman could be a political leader of Muslims to which he replied by quoting the well-known tradition: 'Those who entrust their affairs to a woman will never know prosperity!' In her writings Mernissi points out that women have often had a bad press because so many of the writers have been male. This may have prompted her to write her book on the forgotten queens of Islam in which she chronicles and analyses the histories of remarkable women rulers. She concludes this by reflecting on politics in the modern Islamic scene in which women, although more educated, are often excluded.[5] However, Pakistan, Bangladesh, Turkey and Tunisia provide us with exceptions. The researches of Dr Margaret Smith have also presented us with careful documentation, this time not about forgotten women rulers but about unsung women saints. She wrote her doctoral thesis about the mystic Rabia and the position of women Sufi saints in Islam.[6]

In Islam the question of singleness affects both men and women. There prevails a view that singleness is un-Islamic. According to the Quran marriage is one of God's signs or *ayat* (Q. 30:21). Marriage is represented as a gift of God and the norm for humankind. Some Sufi orders encouraged celibacy for religious reasons. Al-Ghazali commended it if one could not cope with the expenses and burdens of family life. Some non-Sufis, such as Jamal al-Din al-Afghani, also never married. When any admiring disciple offered his daughter as a bride, Jamal al-Din always answered: 'The *ummah* (Islamic community) is my spouse.' There are many examples of well-known Muslim women who never married: such as Fatima Jinnah, the sister of Muhammad Ali Jinnah, the founder of Pakistan. As larger professional middle classes emerge in more and more countries the numbers who choose to remain single increases among Muslim women.

Another question relevant to women is the extent to which prevailing cultural patterns, for example the veiling of women, have been endorsed by Islam although they were not basically Islamic. The Quran clearly does not require total veiling:

'O, Prophet, say to thy wives and thy daughters, and the womenfolks of the believers, that they let down some (part) of their mantles over them; that is more suitable for their being recognised and not insulted. Allah is forgiving, compassionate' (Q. 33:59).[7] The fact that total seclusion and complete veiling is required in some parts of the Muslim world and not in others suggests that custom or fundamentalism or traditional male domination are determining factors. The practice is being challenged today in many lands.

Human Rights

Traditionalists and modernists in Islam are never so divided as on the question of the position and rights of women. New laws relating to the position of women have been introduced in many Muslim lands. Reform laws have often been linked

to a new way of interpreting the Quran. How can a divine
law be amended? In adapting and interpreting Quranic
teaching for the modern world four principles can be observed.
First, a procedural device by which the reformers did not
change the divine law but gave orders that it was not to be
applied. The courts in certain circumstances were not to hear
a case. Second, laws were formulated partly from one school
of law and partly from another or from several. Third, a new
use of consensus or *ijma* has developed, which involves going
back to the original sources and making fresh deductions.
Consensus in Islam means the agreement of the community
of Muslims. Muhammad is reported to have said that his
community would never agree on an error. Finally, administra-
tive orders based on one of the three principles described above,
with something added which is not contrary or repugnant to
Islam, have sometimes made possible the adoption of reforms
even in Islamic states.

Islam often gets a bad press in the West on the subject of
basic human rights. To understand Muslim positions on
human rights we have to look more closely at the Muslim
world view. Islam is God-centred not human-centred. Islamic
social concepts do not separate the individual from the state;
both are part of one system and accountable to God. Secularists
see the need to protect the individual by law so that the state
does not exceed its bounds. Such an idea is foreign to Islam.

According to the United Nations Universal Declaration of
Human Rights Article 2 no distinctions are to be made between
individuals. There is to be equality 'without distinctions of
any kind'. However, the Islamic legal tradition, *fiqh* or jurisprudence, takes distinctions for granted, for example, between
men and women and between Muslims and non-Muslims.
Article 16.1 speaks of 'equal rights as to marriage, during
marriage and its dissolution', but a Muslim woman cannot
marry a non-Muslim man although a Muslim man can marry
a Christian or a Jew. Despite many reforms in the area of
family law relating to women, children and inheritance in
most Muslim countries, the right of divorce for women is
only on certain conditions, which do not apply to men. (We
should note that the UN Declaration has been officially

accepted by most countries, including Islamic states, and states in which Muslims are a majority.) We will deal with UN Article 18 and the subject of freedom of thought, conscience and religion in Chapter 9.

Jihad, or Holy War

Many Westerners challenge the ethical justification for taking up arms in the name of religion. Muslims and Christians have both taken up arms against each other in the names of their respective faiths without due ethical justification. Whatever our perspective, it is important that we understand the Muslim concept of jihad in its ideal definition based on the Quran, the Sunnah and the writings of Muslim theologians.

Maulana Kausar Niazi stressed that Islamic jihad is not directed at expanding the frontiers of the Muslim states. Shedding the blood of innocent people is a heinous crime. Jihad, in terms of military action, only becomes necessary when Muslims are persecuted, their mosques destroyed and their rights trampled upon or when some enemy country invades a Muslim territory.[8] Maulana Muhammad Ali noted that in jihad the first duty – that of inviting people to Islam – is a permanent duty of all Muslims everywhere; while the second duty involving military action arises only in certain contingencies. The Quran speaks of a jihad to attain to Allah: 'And those who strive hard for Us, We will certainly guide them in Our ways' (Q. 29:69).[9] Then it speaks of carrying on a jihad against unbelievers by means of the Holy Quran, which it calls *jihad-an kabir-an* or a very great jihad: 'Strive hard against them a mighty striving with it (the Quran)' (Q. 25:52). Islam's greatest jihad is, therefore, not by means of the sword, but by means of the Quran, a missionary effort to establish Islam. There should always be a party among Muslims who invite people to Islam. 'And from among you there should be a party who invite to good and enjoin what is right and forbid the wrong, and these it is that shall be successful' (Q. 3:103). So the missionary jihad of Islam is to be carried on in all circumstances.[10] Jihad as military warfare is limited to defined situations and should only be declared by a spiritual leader of integrity. This ideal has not always prevailed but the teaching is clear.

Conclusion

Ziauddin Sardar in his article entitled 'The Ethical Connection: Christian-Muslim Relations in the Postmodern Age' comments that, 'The survival of believers as believers, in an increasingly meaningless postmodern world, depends on tackling some of the great social, political and intellectual issues of our time on the basis of a joint ethical programme that draws its conceptual and value parameters from the monotheistic sources of Islam and Christianity.'[11] Undoubtedly there are areas in which Muslims and Christians, as people of faith, can co-operate. The difficulty, however, with Ziauddin Sardar's assessment is that while the Quran and the Bible have clear teaching on ethics the bases are different. Christian ethics are based on the Bible's call to love God and love our neighbour (Deuteronomy 6:5 and Leviticus 19:18). Christ's incarnation, death and resurrection embody that call and the Holy Spirit provides the power to obey the command. With this the Muslim is unlikely to agree. Although there is a passionate concern for justice in both the Quran and the Bible the ethical bases of the two faiths have different foundations grounded in their different conceptions of the nature of God.

1. *Islam and Ecology* (Cassell, 1992).
2. Professor Omran is a world authority on population, health and Islamic studies, and founder of the World Association of Muslim Scholars for Population, Health and Development.
3. Professor of Sociology at the Institut Universitaire de la Recherche Scientifique, Université Mohammed V in Rabat, Morocco.
4. *Women in Islam: An Historical and Theological Enquiry* (Blackwell, 1991).
5. *The Forgotten Queens of Islam* (Polity Press, 1993).
6. *Rabi'a the Mystic and her Fellow-Saints* (Cambridge University Press, 1984).

7. *The Qur'an,* tr. Richard Bell (T. & T. Clark, 1960), vol. 11.
8. *Islam Our Guide* (S. Muhammad Ashraf, 1976), p. 20.
9. *The Meaning of the Glorious Qur'an,* tr. Abdullah Yusif Ali (2 vols., Dar Al-Kitab Al-Misri, Cairo, 1938).
10. Muhammad Ali, *A Manual of Hadith* (Curzon Press, 1983), pp. 252–3.
11. *Islam and Christian-Muslim Relations,* vol. 2, no. 1, June 1991, p. 56.

8

Religious Structures

Islamic Institutions

The establishment of Muslim institutions is integral to Islam. These include the mosque, the mosque school, the shrine, the Islamic seminary, the legislative system, the Muslim university and the Islamic cultural centre.

Mosque

Wherever Muslims go, mosques spring up. If twelve or more men, including a prayer leader, meet regularly in a certain place for daily prayers together for a year they may claim that this is prayer territory and cannot be used for other purposes. In Pakistan such claims were made concerning a small area in the middle of a college sports field and a mosque was duly constructed. In the UK as the numbers of Muslims have increased so have the mosques. Many of them are small and function in private houses with the sitting-rooms permanently set apart for the purpose of prayer. Others are large and modern like the Central Mosque at Regent's Park, London, or the main mosque in Birmingham. In 1966 there were eighteen registered mosques. By 1976 the number had increased to 119 and in 1985 the total was 338.[1] The mosque is not only the location for daily and Friday communal prayers but it is a social and community centre, mainly for men. The preacher who gives the sermon at noon prayers on Fridays is generally a mullah or maulvi attached to the mosque. He is likely to have some other way of earning or subsidising his livelihood. Although the impression is sometimes given that there are Muslim clerics it is not strictly correct. In Islam there is no distinction between clergy and laity, despite the fact that mullahs may have done many years of Arabic and theological studies. There is no 'ordination' as there is in most Christian denominations.

The mosque school
The mosque school or *madrasah* is a mosque-related educational institution for the training of children or future religious leadership. It generally functions in the early morning and evening when schoolchildren are free. The teaching, usually done by a mullah, mainly consists of learning classical Arabic and memorisation of the Arabic Quran, preferably the whole of it.

Theological colleges
There are many theological colleges connected with mosques where men train and then on graduating are attached to mosques either as prayer leaders or preachers, the former being attached to a particular mosque and the second going to any mosque where they are invited. Recently, when I was touring with a friend in North-West China, we visited several mosques in Urumchi and Kashgar which had theological schools and libraries attached. Generally the student numbers were under twenty. Arabic and studies of the Quran and Traditions featured prominently in the curriculum, which seemed similar to that used in the Indian subcontinent.

Shrines and holy persons
Shrines are dotted all over most Muslim countries. Muslim immigrants in Europe keep in close touch with their roots and will combine visits back to the lands of their origin for weddings and funerals with a visit to their family holy man called a *shaikh* or *marabout* in Arabic or a *pir* in Urdu. It is generally a man (rarely a woman), who is connected with a shrine either because he is a descendant of the revered founder of the shrine or because he is revered for his saintliness, powers of healing, counselling or miracle-working and has himself established the shrine. Sometimes the shrine-keepers are not related to the dead saint but a certain family looks after the

shrine and this job passes from generation to generation. Theology is not particularly the saint's department, but some of the well-known holy men have a resident theologian as part of their back-up personnel. (This is the case in the large shrine of Golrah Sharif just outside Rawalpindi in Pakistan.) A shrine generally has a mosque attached or nearby. People often go to shrines when they are ill and women go when they are barren. In the hospital where I lived for fifteen years in the North West Frontier Province of Pakistan many of the patients had sought healing at shrines. Sometimes the holy man told them to go to the hospital when they did not find healing at the shrine.

Once, near Pune in India, together with some friends, I visited the shrine and tomb of Sufi Qamar Ali Darvesh at a village called Shivapur, which was near a spring with medicinal qualities. Pilgrims came from far and near to seek healing in the name of the saint, to drink the spring water and to witness the saint's miracles or *karamat*. We watched the phenomenon of the levitating rocks. Two large round boulders lay close to each other. The larger, weighing about 70 kg, was raised to a height of nearly 2 metres for several minutes by eleven men using only an index finger each, and calling in unison on the name of the saint. Not only the illiterate and untaught are involved in saint veneration. Benazir Bhutto in her autobiography wrote that before her father's execution he had urged her to pray at the shrine of Lal Shahbaz Qalander, one of their most famous saints. 'My grandmother had gone to pray at his shrine when my father became very ill as a baby and nearly died. Would God be able to hear a daughter's prayer for the same person?'[2]

Exorcism is another healing role found in many parts of the world. In Muscat, the capital of the Sultanate of Oman, I have heard Muslim exorcists at work for hours in the evening and earlier part of the night attempting to cast out evil spirits. To listen to the chanting of the exorcists and the shrieks of the afflicted is an eerie and chilling experience. Religious teachers or mullahs were probably engaged in this work but I could not be sure of their status. I have heard of those who have claimed deliverance but I had no first-hand knowledge of their previous state. Some consider, and others corroborate, that they are possessed by evil jinn. The figure of the healer in many Muslim countries is more often the saint and the religious teacher than the scientifically trained doctor.

Islamic Universities and Seminaries

Al-Azhar, Cairo, Egypt

The most famous institution for academic and theological training is the Al-Azhar in Cairo. It is one of the oldest universities in the world and was founded in 970 by the Shias. After two centuries it became the centre of Sunni Islam and remains so today. Through a special law in 1961 it was fundamentally reorganised. New faculties were formed for medicine, agriculture, engineering and commerce. Its graduates take jobs all over the world, and spread Islam as they follow their chosen professions. Increasingly it receives students from other countries who are sent for further training as religious leaders. An acquaintance of mine did a three-year course at the Al-Azhar, sponsored by his government with the purpose of returning to his country to train religious leaders. Its Academy of Islamic Research promotes the work of Muslim scholars all over the world.

Deoband, Saharanpur, India

An Islamic seminary in Deoband, a small town about a hundred miles north of Delhi, was founded in 1867 by two classically trained religious scholars. Those connected with the seminary were called Deobandis. The influence of the Deobandis is still perpetuated in North India and has reached the UK.

Deobandis followed the Hanafi school of law, and were conservative and traditional at a time of considerable Western influence which they rejected in their thinking and curriculum. They were also pietist, reformed in their Sufism and opposed to the shrine-cult. Through Urdu, the main language of the Muslims of India, they endeavoured to spread their teaching using not only their graduates but also the press, mail service and the railway system.

Bareilly, Uttar Pradesh, India

A parallel movement, to become known as the Barelwi movement, was started by a scholarly member of the Qadiri Sufi
brotherhood, Ahmad Raza Khan (1856–1921), in North India.
Through his scholarship he acted as an advocate for the world
of the shrine and *pir*. In this and in some theological points
about the mystical knowledge of God this movement differed
from the Deobandis. Through the years much contention has
been generated between the two groups which sometimes flares
up today. Tablighi Jamaat activities (see below) are banned
in Barelwi mosques even now.[3]

Bury and Dewsbury seminaries, UK

The Deobandi seminaries, established in Bury in 1975 and in
Dewsbury in 1982, strengthen links with Deobandi mosques
around the UK and there is much interaction all round. Leaders
for Muslims in Britain, numbering under twenty in each
institution, are trained over a period of six (Bury) or seven
years (Dewsbury) in both seminaries. There is some interchange
of teaching staff. The curriculum includes memorising the whole
of the Quran, exegetical studies and studies of the traditions.
Some graduates do further studies at the Al-Azhar in Cairo.
Students who have some South Asian language as their mother
tongue, and learn Arabic at seminary, using Urdu as the medium
of instruction, often find it very difficult to relate in the English-
speaking environment of the UK, both linguistically and
culturally. This is gradually changing but the problem remains
of adequate financial resources for graduates in their mosque
leadership and secular employment.

The world assembly of the Tablighi Jamaat (preaching party)
was held at Dewsbury in June 1994. This was the largest
gathering of Muslims in the UK. The Tablighi Jamaat was
started by a lecturer of Deoband who resigned to start a movement more rooted in the needs of nominal Muslims but which
remained within the Deobandi tradition. It called for full
participation of all Muslims in door-to-door revivalism. I once
met a team of six members of the Tablighi Jamaat on a bus in
Pakistan. They were returning from a religious convention
in the Northern Areas and travelling back to their headquarters

in Raiwind. Their leader asked me to look after their luggage while they got out at every five-minute stop on the long journey to talk to individuals around the bus stops about their commitment to the practice of Islam.

Other Religious Structures

Islamic cultural centres

Saudi Arabia provides financial support for Muslims in other parts of the world to establish mosques with extensive cultural centres attached. For West Africa the centre is in Liberia, for North Africa it is in the Algerian city of Constantine, with its lovely complex including a theological school. Muslim architecture is generally impressive and the new cultural centre in Hong Kong is a modern example. Plenty of free literature was available there. When I visited with a group of students we were most courteously received by the mosque authorities and shown round and then given an interesting brief talk about Islam, with special reference to Hong Kong and China. This was followed by the opportunity to ask questions.

Shariah or Islamic law

A legislative system and an economic structure based on the Shariah or Islamic law is regarded by some Muslims as desirable where Muslims are in the majority. For example, Nizam-e-Mustafa, or the ordering of society according to the way of the Prophet Muhammad, was introduced into Pakistan by President Zia ul-Haq. One result was that Islamic banking was practised with the elimination of usury, as demanded in the Quran. Islamic banking is based on the idea that all participants should share profits and losses. My small savings account in Pakistan became a profit and loss account and I received bonuses instead of interest. However, it has proved more difficult to apply Islamic banking principles in international trade. Arabic replaced English as the second language in the state schools. There were also calls for the repeal of the Family Laws Ordinance of 1961 and women experienced greater restrictions in dress and legal rights. Whether the testimony of one woman equalled that of one man in the courts was questioned. It was finally left to the judge in each particular case to decide if one or two women's testimony equalled that of one man. In 1988 the Shariah Ordinance was introduced to deal with a limited agenda. Most matters came under the jurisdiction of civil rather than Shariah courts. However, in 1991 the Shariah Act was passed, making death the punishment for blaspheming the Prophet Muhammad. There has been ample publicity about this in the world press as well as over the fatwa pronounced on the British author Salman Rushdie by Ayatollah Khomeini in 1989 for writing the novel *The Satanic Verses,* which he considered blasphemous. Khomeini regarded his Islamic Revolution in Iran as a world movement and therefore considered that he had jurisdiction over Salman Rushdie who was born a Muslim. Rushdie has been living under police protection ever since, as, despite the Ayatollah's death, no one has dared to revoke the fatwa calling for the writer's death, although Khomeini's authority was, according to many Islamic scholars, limited to his lifetime.

Recognised Roles for Men

Prophet or rasul
According to the Quran the six greatest prophets or *rasul* are Adam, Noah, Abraham, Moses, Isa (Jesus) and Muhammad. A *rasul* is an apostle of Allah, that is, someone on whom Allah has sent down his message or *rasalat*; therefore, he is a messenger of God. The Muslim concept of prophethood does not imply foretelling but simply reciting what has been sent down from God. The prophet does not influence the message but simply declares it in order to bring humankind back to the ideal religion. Prophethood ended with Muhammad.

Imam
We have seen how the Shias see the specialised role of the imam. The Sunnis understand an imam to be a local religious leader who will probably also be a mosque leader. He may represent the local Muslim community in civic affairs.

Ulama

Ulama are Islamic theologians and scholars. *Ulama* is the plural of *alim,* who may also be called mullah, maulvi or maulana especially in the Indian subcontinent. Their training is often limited to Arabic and Quranic studies.

Ayatollah

Allama al-Hilli (d. 1325) was the first Shia scholar to bear the name Ayatollah (which in Arabic means God's sign). He held that through reasoning the jurist was capable of giving valid judgment even in religious matters. Thus al-Hilli paved the way for the later political role of the Shia scholars called mullahs and ayatollahs. Because of their infallibility neither Muhammad nor the imams could use individual enquiry or *ijtihad.* The Prophet had to wait until a revelation came to him and the imams had to depend on instruction from the Prophet or on divine inspiration. Because *ijtihad* was fallible, restricted to a living authority and could be revised, legal rulings were flexible, dynamic and could be revised. Infallible authority was reserved for the Hidden Imam in a distant future so the company of his fallible representatives, the scholars, could now devote themselves to the practical task of handling current questions without being too tied to the authority of the written word. In fact the Shia *mujtahids* – the ayatollahs of today – are anything but fundamentalist.[4]

Some Roles for Women

Women in religious leadership

Very many women follow Sufi saints or *pirs* today especially in South Asia, and some are leaders. Among the Sufis the distinction between male and female tends to disappear. A woman may be a top-ranking saint. Rabia is one of the most famous of all Sufi saints. Giuseppe Scattolin in his article on 'Women in Islamic Mysticism'[5] writes that Sufi women are rarely mentioned in the common manuals on Sufism, except for Rabia. However, Ibn al-Jawzi (d. 1200) recorded in his *Sifat al-Safwa* the names of more than two hundred ascetic and Sufi women, and Abd al-Rauf al-Munawi (d. 1621) in his *Al-Kawakib al-durriya* gives biographical account of thirty-five of them. Most of these Sufi women belonged to the first and second generation of Islam, in which ascetic Sufism was prevalent. The majority of these Sufi women were also endowed with supernatural powers and miracles or *karamat* and became respected and recognised teachers, and even leaders of religious communities.

Women in political leadership

One debating point about the position of women in Muslim lands is whether a woman can be head of state or not. In Pakistan in 1964 Miss Fatima Jinnah, sister of the late Quaid-i-Azam, Muhammad Ali Jinnah, was candidate of the Combined Opposition Parties opposing President Ayub Khan who was campaigning for re-election. At that time some Pakistani Muslim theologians (*ulama*) made a pronouncement (fatwa) that a woman can be head of state in an Islamic state. Maulana Maududi, having agreed with the pronouncement, later changed his view and stated that a woman could not occupy a position of responsibility. This statement can be interpreted as denying to a woman the right to hold the office of a minister of state or the headship of an institution or even the right to vote. In support of the opposite view Maulana Kausar Niazi pointed out that Ibn Hazm (d. 1064) considers that a woman can hold all posts except that of caliph.[6] She can now be head of a Muslim state as the Caliphate is defunct. When Benazir Bhutto became Prime Minister of Pakistan in 1988 she was acclaimed the first Muslim woman head of government. Bangladesh and Turkey have also elected women Muslim Prime Ministers. In *Sultanes Oubliées, Chefs d'Etat en Islam* (Paris, 1990: *Forgotten Sultanas, Women Heads of State in Islam*), Professor Mernissi describes women who played a prominent role in Islamic history. Sultana Radia ruled in Delhi after overthrowing her despotic brother in the thirteenth century. Yemen had several Muslim women queens, including Malika Urwas who ruled for nearly fifty years in the eleventh century. There were at least four queens in Indonesia in the seventeenth century. Professor Mernissi in her extensive researches has unearthed details of other Muslim queens which have been ignored by most Arab male historians.

Relationships to Government Structures and Authority

Relationships to government structures vary even within countries which have large Muslim majorities. Indonesia has the largest Muslim population in the world but is not an Islamic state. Turkey has a secular constitution but through some of its political parties Islamic influence is growing very fast. In some Middle Eastern countries, notably in Saudi Arabia, Egypt, Jordan, Syria, the influence of the religious police is evident. Their function is to monitor religious activities especially those of non-Muslims and to check up on the practice of Muslims. They are particularly active in ensuring that the Ramadan fast is kept. In Saudi Arabia anyone – Muslim or non-Muslim – caught eating or drinking during that month is imprisoned. Some Muslim countries have a special Minister for Religious Affairs. Maulana Kausar Niazi held such a position in Pakistan. He was Minister for Religious Affairs, Hajj and Auqaf. The portfolio includes responsibility for the pilgrimage arrangements for Pakistanis to go Mecca – special hajj flights etc. Another responsibility includes the collection of religious taxes and their use as well as overall oversight of all Muslim religious buildings and sites within the country. All this comes under *auqaf*. On the international scene Islamic summit conferences involving heads of state continue to be held. International gatherings for a multitude of issues and agendas proliferate.

1. Jørgen Nielsen, *Muslims in Western Europe* (Edinburgh University Press, 1992), p. 45.
2. *Daughter of the East* (Mandarin, 1988), p. 142.
3. Philip Lewis, *Islamic Britain* (I. B. Tauris, 1994), p. 40.
4. See Heinz Hamm, *Shiism* (Edinburgh University Press, 1991), p. 71.
5. *Encounter* no. 198, Oct. 1993.
6. Kausar Niazi, *Modern Challenges to Muslim Families.*

Propagating the Faith

Islamic Mission or *Dawah*

To the Muslim Islam is essentially global. As the first surah of the Quran says, Allah is 'Lord of the Worlds', meaning Lord of this world and the next. Islam divides this world into two sections: the house of Islam or *dar al-Islam* – that part of the world which submits to Allah – and the house of war or *dar al-harb* – that part of the world which has yet to be brought into submission or obedience to Allah. A Muslim state based on Shariah or Islamic law is the house of Islam; everywhere else is the house of war. Westerners find it hard to understand that for the Muslim there is no sacred and secular. Religion and politics can never be separated, hence Islam is a missionary faith.

The concept of mission in Islam is called *dawah* in Arabic. Its basic meaning is 'a call' or 'an invitation', and, in specialised usage, 'missionary activity'. This idea comes in the Quran in surah 16:125: 'Call unto the way of thy Lord with wisdom and fair exhortation, and reason with them in the better way'. A minority sees active mission as a religious duty for all, even though the activists are not agreed on the extent of *dawah*. It is not limited to the 'calling' of non-Muslims exclusively. There is always the challenge for the Muslim to be fully Muslim. The double responsibility of *dawah* for every Muslim is to be renewed in his *islam* or submission to God and to help his fellow-Muslims in this, and to 'invite' non-Muslims to embrace Islam.

Muslims in a minority in North America and Europe have

tended to stress the importance of building mosques and distributing the Quran and other literature as a convincing way of fulfilling *dawah*. There is an attempt to adapt to the majority culture. For example, in a large mosque in Los Angeles I once attended Friday noon prayers in which many women were taking part, sitting behind the men. In the Middle East and Asia I have never witnessed this large participation by women. On that occasion about sixty black Americans became Muslims by reciting the creed. The majority were women from a nominally Christian (Baptist) background who were attracted to Islam by its discipline and strict moral family code.

Korea – A Case History

We can take the establishing of a Muslim minority in the Republic of Korea as a case-study of *dawah*. In 1955 there were no Korean Muslims. Two Turks, serving with the United Nations forces, felt their personal obligation to spread Islam and started to preach its message to refugees of the Korean War. A hut was built for use as a mosque. The development of Islam in the country is outlined in a booklet entitled *Islam in Korea*, produced by the Korea Muslim Federation and available at the mosque in Seoul.

Next a Korea Muslim society was formed with an elected imam and president. Some of the Korean Muslims were sent to a Muslim college in Malaysia to be trained as future Islamic workers and leaders. Even so it was not easy to make a base for *dawah*. The Korean Government approved and officially registered the Korea Islamic Foundation, and in 1974 the Seoul Central Masjid and Islamic Centre was built. To promote effective *dawah* work through education the Korea-Saudi Arabia Joint Committee was formed to establish the Korean Islamic College. The Korean Government donated the site.

Through many seminars on 'Dawah in the Minority Islamic Countries' and 'Dawah in Rural Districts' Korean Muslims are preparing for effective *dawah*. In 1978 132 persons went on the pilgrimage to Mecca. Each year since 1979 an Islamic Cultural Exhibition has been held in Seoul. The spread of

Islam was hindered by an insufficient understanding of Korean culture by the missionaries sent out and, the fact that Friday, the day for special noon prayers, is a work day in Korea. A lack of adequate educational material about Islam is an added reason for the hesitation of Koreans to accept Islam.

The involvement of so many Korean workers in the oil countries of the Middle East has raised the interest in Islam among the Koreans. Today there are more than 33,000 Korean Muslims and mosques in six major cities. Some Koreans, as well as those of other nationalities, have become Muslims, through their exposure to *dawah* during their employment in Saudi Arabia and other Middle Eastern Muslim states.

Europe – A Strategy

In considering Islam's global strategy we could look at its plans for one continent as given in a brochure prepared for widespread distribution.

> The Islamic Council of Europe was established in 1973 . . . in implementation of two resolutions adopted by the Second and Third Conferences of Foreign Ministers held in Jiddah (Saudi Arabia) and Benghazi (the Libyan Arab Republic) respectively . . . The Islamic Council of Europe is the supreme co-ordinating body for Islamic Centres and organisations in Europe. It is an independent organisation, but acts in close co-operation with International Islamic organisations (and) the Governments of all the Muslim states . . . It has its Headquarters in London and constituents in almost every country of Europe. Among its stated Objectives are:
>
> ● To assist, support and supplement the activities of the member organisations in different fields of the present day, including establishment of mosques and Muslim cultural centres, dissemination of Islamic education, and fulfilment of other Islamic duties and obligations.
> ● To make necessary arrangements for the establishment

of new centres for organised Islamic activity wherever necessary.

● To seek the co-operation and assistance of Muslim states, national governments and national and international organisations, in the promotion of the activities of the Council and its constituents.

Resources for Islamic Mission

Nearly half the world's known oil resources lie in the Middle East. Saudi Arabia uses much of its wealth strategically to spread the faith of Islam. The world's most powerful radio transmitter, called the Voice of Islam, and the largest printing works are located in Saudi Arabia. It publishes twenty-eight million copies of the Quran in various languages each year. International gatherings of various kinds are often held in Saudi Arabia. Muslim summit conferences, financed mainly by Saudi money, are held in different cities of the Islamic world.

Reasons for Embracing Islam

In his recent article entitled 'Post-Conversion Experiences of Native British Converts to Islam', Ali Köse comes to various conclusions from his formal interviews with seventy converts. Unfortunately in the article he does not mention on what basis the seventy were chosen. All of them came from Christian backgrounds except for three from Jewish ones. Fifty-one were Anglicans. They all experienced deep changes in belief, practices and life style, and 81 per cent took Islamic names. 'For them, Islam meant finding the end of the line started by the Prophet Abraham, not rejection of the Judeo-Christian tradition.'[1] Ali Köse also underlines the importance of how the new community of faith provides for the ongoing sponsorship of the new convert in providing 'affirmation, encouragement, guidance and models'.[2]

The Times published an editorial and several articles and letters about British women who had converted to Islam. The editorial entitled 'Choosing Islam' listed several reasons for the attractiveness of Islam to Western women. One is its intellectual clarity and moral certainty for those disillusioned by the moral relativity of their own culture. 'Though some are converting to Islam after marrying Pakistani or Bangladeshi men, others are making the leap of faith as an independent act of spiritual self-improvement.'[3] A further attraction is the sense of sisterhood and community they find in Islam. Others are attracted by aspects of Islamic culture and especially by Muslim architecture and the beauty of classical Arabic.

Muhtar Holland, the translator of Al-Ghazali's *On the Duties of Brotherhood,* gives a brief account as to why he became a Muslim.

> When I came to feel the need to espouse a religion (meaning to commit myself to one 'for better or worse', as opposed to flirting with religiousness on the one hand, or to nominal membership from birth on the other), it was Islam that I chose to embrace . . . As for the choice of Islam, one consideration was the directness and blazing simplicity of its doctrine: I could see truth in other religions, but here the Truth was plainest *to me.* The second consideration was the Islamic emphasis on brotherhood.[4]

Factors in the Spread of Islam

Historically we can trace the factors contributing to the spread of Islam. Political alliances and military conquests included provision for those who did not accept Islam. They were given special status as *ahl al-dhimma* or protected people. In the Quran Jews and Christians were given special status in relation to Muslims as *ahl al-kitab* or People of the Book, although it is not clear exactly what this status was. Trade was another factor in the early expansion of Islam. The traders themselves may have not been particularly zealous in the propagation of their faith but they were accompanied or followed by Muslim religious teachers who nurtured both the traders in the caravans and the newly established commercial communities.

Slowly non-Muslims were influenced by Islamic practices, and subsequently by Islamic beliefs, and Islam spread. Sufism, with its piety and devotion, contributed much to the spread of Islam. One of the strengths of Sufism was that through its brotherhoods it could permeate areas where Islam did not yet rule, as it was not linked to political structures.

In the eighteenth and nineteenth centuries new historical situations developed, especially in Western Europe. The Ottoman Empire, weakened by internal dissension, was now faced with external threats as well. Far from being able to continue the world mission of Islam, Muslims were faced with the prospect of losing much of what they had acquired during the original expansion. In Eastern Europe, North Africa, the Middle East, and the Indian subcontinent, the orientation changed from offensive to defensive and remained so in most Muslim countries until quite recently. The acquisition of independence by so many countries with Muslim majorities and the economic power that oil has given have led to the more confident and aggressive approaches of groups like the Muslim Brotherhood and Jamaat-i Islami.

Al-Ikhwan al-Muslimun or the Muslim Brothers (generally known outside the Arabic speaking world as the Muslim Brotherhood) was founded in 1928 by Hasan al-Banna (1906–49), an Egyptian schoolteacher who was deeply influenced by Sufism. He wanted to work more practically than was possible through the mosque or the Sufi brotherhoods so he founded what was at first a student organisation. He sent students to the coffee shops and other public meeting places to preach Islam. He used individuals to reach individuals and was remarkably effective especially among civil servants, clerks, teachers and professionals. The Brotherhood's four main goals were: to make every individual a true Muslim, to develop the Muslim family on Islamic lines, to establish a Muslim community or *ummah*, and to establish an Islamic state in Egypt. The Brotherhood is now active in all Arabic-speaking countries and takes a significant part in influencing political situations, sometimes using violence.

Jamaat-i Islami became the counterpart to the Muslim Brotherhood in the non-Arabic speaking world. It was founded

by Abul Ala Maududi (1903–79), a journalist born in India
who was also influenced by Sufism. He opposed the formation
of Pakistan but emigrated there to press for a more clearly
defined Islamic state. He wrote that his *dawah* was to all
people but to Muslims especially. Transformed individual
Muslims were to be the basis for the transforming of society.
He advocated an austere life style with a focus on winning
the blessings of the world to come. On founding the Jamaat-
i Islami in 1941 he also addressed political and social matters.
He did not call for revolution or violence but stressed preaching
and an extensive use of literature. His movement was politically
orientated and soon became a political party with the objective
of attaining political power in the newly created Pakistan
(1947).

Attitude to Christianity's Missionary Mandate

Muslim attitudes to Christianity's missionary mandate today
depend on whether Muslims are in the majority or minority
in the state, and on whether the state is Muslim or secular.
Sometimes there is misunderstanding by both Muslims and
Christians of what the Church's missionary mandate is. The
Bible teaches that God loves each person, not just those who
love him. The Apostle Paul wrote: 'God demonstrates his own
love for us in this: While we were still sinners Christ died for
us' (Romans 5:8). In Luke 4:18–19 Jesus Christ quoted the
prophet Isaiah to define his mandate:

> The Spirit of the Lord is on me,
> because he has anointed me
> to preach good news to the poor.
> He has sent me to proclaim freedom for the prisoners
> and recovery of sight for the blind,
> to release the oppressed,
> to proclaim the year of the Lord's favour.

It included preaching, teaching, healing and establishing justice.
In many parts of the world Muslims have welcomed Christian

schools and medical work. More recently they have endorsed the holistic approach of Christians to relief and development work by engaging in such work themselves using similar models. Some Muslim governments have felt threatened by Christian activities. Malaysia bans any book which deals with both Christian and Muslim themes. Some countries are not willing to receive foreign Christian workers although the nationally recognised churches in those countries, aware of their international family, are willing and happy to do so.

Religious Toleration and Human Rights in Islam

When Muslims are in a majority those of other religions sometimes experience pressure and lack of freedom in the profession, practice and propagation of their faith. This is most commonly true of Christians. In Sudan, for example, there is persecution of Christians on a large scale, as was highlighted by the visit in 1994 of the Archbishop of Canterbury.

Individual Muslims who change their allegiance from Islam to Christianity often experience great pressure. In Egypt, where there has been a large Christian community from long before the rise of Islam, this problem is growing. Equal treatment of all citizens and a commitment to freedom of religious belief is guaranteed by Article 40 of Egypt's 1971 Constitution. There is a dichotomy between apparent application of civil law and the actual implementation of Islamic law. This was highlighted in an interview with the Supreme Court Justice Said Al-Ashmawi.[5] He stated: 'It is understood that converting from another faith to Islam is approved, while converting from Islam to another faith is prevented . . . I hold that Egyptian law is actually Islamic law.'[6] Article 18 of the Universal Declaration of Human Rights provides that 'Every person has the right to freedom of thought, conscience and religion. This right includes the right to change his religion or belief.' Egypt has ratified the International Covenant on Civil and Political Rights (which enforces the Universal Declaration). However, Muslim converts to Christ in Egypt may not change their identity papers to reflect their conversion to a new religion.

The position of those who convert to Islam according to the Quran

While the idea of freedom to become a Muslim is warmly accepted by Muslim governments, the freedom to leave Islam is not often recognised. In Islam individual freedom of expression is generally allowed if it contributes to the benefit of all. Since the Quran teaches that 'there is no compulsion in religion' (Q. 2:256) and distinguishes between belief based on personal conviction and formal acceptance of Islam (Q. 49:14), the state should not enforce Islam. There is an implied tolerance in these words: 'Unto you your religion, and unto me mine', addressed to Meccan idolaters (Q. 109:6). Muhammad was a warner, with no authority to convert forcibly. Quran 10:100 states: 'And if thy Lord had willed, all who are in the earth could have believed together.'

Apostasy

A key verse about how Muslims should deal with those who renounce the faith of Islam is:

> They long that ye should disbelieve even as they disbe-
> lieve, that ye may be upon a level (with them). So choose
> not friends from them till they forsake their home in the
> way of Allah; if they turn back (to enmity) then take them
> and kill them wherever ye find them, and choose no friend
> nor helper from among them . . .' (Q. 4:89).

Muslim commentaries show that in its original context it is not concerned with Muslims becoming Christians but with those who were known as 'Hypocrites' – idolaters who made a profession of Islam, but were not sincere and later went back to their former way of life. The *hadith* literature contains a variety of sayings of the Prophet about apostasy, and it is here that we find references to the death penalty. Al-Bukhari, recognised as the most authoritative collector of *hadith*, relates that 'the Prophet said: "He who forsakes his religion, kill him." '[7] The four schools of Islamic jurisprudence have un-animously agreed on punishment by death in the case of apostasy. There is a real tension, if not an inconsistency, between the traditional Islamic responses to conversion and the UN Universal Declaration of Human Rights. The most significant test of Muslim attitudes to conversion, however, is not the statements of jurists and theologians of the past and present, but what actually happens in practice. However liberal and tolerant Muslim leaders can be, what seems to count most is the attitude of a particular family to any member who seems to be rejecting Islam and bringing dishonour on the whole family. In this there are a variety of reactions, ranging from the supreme penalty to leniency.

1. *Islam & Christian-Muslim Relations*, vol. 2, no. 5, 1995.
2. Ibid., p. 200.
3. *The Times,* 10 Nov. 1993.
4. *On the Duties of Brotherhood*, tr. Muhtar Holland (Latimer New Dimensions Ltd., 1975), foreword, p. 11.
5. *The Application of Islamic Jurisprudence in Egypt*, July 1991.
6. *Egypt's Converts* (Middle East Concern, 1995).
7. *The Codification of Islamic Law* (Al-Azhar University, 1982).

Concluding Reflections

Woven into the design of an unusual carpet in the United
Nations building in New York are some words of the poet
Saadi, who came from the lovely city of Shiraz in Iran. Here
is an English translation of the Persian poetry:

> All men are members of the same body,
> Created from one essence.
> If fate brings suffering to one member
> The others cannot stay at rest.
> You who remain indifferent to the burden of pain of others
> Do not deserve to be called human.

If we can accept our common humanity we can relate to our
neighbours as equals. We are basically human and after that
Muslim, Christian, Marxist, or whatever.

In crisis most people pray. Bishop Kenneth Cragg in the
preface to his book *Alive to God,* about Christian and Muslim
prayer, is more specific about our common humanity when
he writes: 'In its deepest quality the will to pray is simply
being human seriously and inclusively. It is being alive
imaginatively'.[1]

It belongs with the genesis of this anthology to believe that
prayer, in whatever camp of faith, is a calling of increasing
puzzlement to contemporary men. Many are at ease neither
in letting it go, nor in letting it stay. They cannot renounce
prayer, any more than they can cease to care about the
world. But they cannot well sustain it, in any sure confidence

about traditional forms and phrases. All such, we might say, are praying to pray – no more, no less . . .[2]

If, whoever we may be, we are concerned with human relationships we must stress our common humanity and experience it in the mosaic of peoples which makes up our populations. The extraordinary dispersing of peoples in our world, from whatever cause, together with the relative ease of global travel give us an unprecedented opportunity to understand and relate to people of many kinds and many persuasions. All human encounters can be enriching. Let us understand our world and then let us look again at Islam with its many faces and at Muslims who are so rich in their diversity.

In a privately circulated letter a friend of mine recently wrote about 'post-modernism' in the West today:

> We are moving from the rationalism and materialism that has prevailed for a hundred years, to a kind of unreason, where there is no absolute truth or ethical standards. People do not believe nothing – they will believe anything that seems to offer to fill the spiritual void. The post-modern mind is marked by its gullibility. It is a new paganism . . . I believe that the challenge to the church in the future is to offer a rational spirituality – a faith in God that is based on objective reality, one which has its emotional expression, but in which subjective feelings are not uppermost.[3]

Some have perhaps come to think of Muslims in terms of fundamentalism and terrorism, and nationalism and holy war or jihad. Fundamentalism is not always about terrorism, more often it is about going back to the fundamentals. Jihad is not always about warfare, more often it is about striving in the way of God with the sword undrawn. Even the militant Muslim fundamentalist may feel on the defensive and be reacting to the modern scene at one extreme, while Salman Rushdie, as a post-modernist novelist, is reacting at the other extreme. They are both Muslims engaging with the secular, pluralist, disintegrating Western world and seeking answers. E. M. Forster said, 'I do not believe in belief.' Rushdie echoes this when he declares: 'I believe in no god', and 'where there is no belief there is no blasphemy'.[4]

Let a convinced Muslim speak. Professor Akbar S. Ahmed dedicates his fascinating book *Postmodernism and Islam: Predicament and Promise* to his two-year-old daughter, Nafees. He concludes his preface thus:

> Nafees will live, as a Muslim, in the postmodern world which is just beginning to shape our lives; therein lies the Muslim predicament: that of living by Islam in an age which is increasingly secular, cynical, irreverent, fragmented, materialistic and, therefore, for a Muslim, often hostile. In an age of cynicism and disintegration Islam has much to offer. I, therefore, pray she finds inspiration in her faith and culture, to assist her in making sense of, and resolving, the predicament of living as a good, caring and decent human being in the postmodernist world.

He speaks as a Muslim for whom Islam covers every aspect of life. For the Christian as well belief should cover every aspect of life. Truth and morality are not relative but absolute. For me it is the Christian faith which claims every aspect of my living and my dying. From a biblical perspective I see no need for competition, estrangement or hostility between Muslims and Christians or between Muslims and Christians and those of other convictions. I believe in the uniqueness of the revelation of God in Christ but I always want to share this faith in love and humility.

1. *Alive to God* (Oxford University Press, 1970), p. vii.
2. Ibid., pp. 40–5.
3. Reverend Canon John Meadowcroft, 1995.
4. 'In Good Faith', *The Independent on Sunday*, 4 Feb. 1990.

Selected Bibliography

Ahmed, Akbar S., *Postmodernism and Islam: Predicament and Promise* (Routledge, 1992).

Al-Ghazali, *Mishat Al-Anwar (The Niche for Lights)* tr. W. H. T. Gairdner (Kitab Bhavan, 1981).

—— *On the Duties of Brotherhood*, tr. Muhtar Holland (Latimer New Dimensions Ltd., 1975).

Ali, Muhammad, *A Manual of Hadith* (Curzon Press, London and Dublin, 1944, reprinted 1983).

Altorki, Soraya, *Women in Saudi Arabia: Ideology and Behavior among the Elite* (Columbia University Press, 1986).

Arberry, A. J., *The Koran Interpreted* (Oxford University Press, 1972).

Bhutto, Benazir, *Daughter of the East* (Mandarin, 1988).

Boswell, C. E., *The Islamic Dynasties* (Edinburgh University Press, 1967).

Burnett, David, *Clash of Worlds* (MARC, 1990).

Carey, George, *The Gate of Glory* (Hodder and Stoughton, 1986).

Chapman, Colin, *Cross and Crescent* (Inter-Varsity Press, 1995).

Cooper, Anne (comp.), *Ishmael my Brother: A Christian Introduction to Islam* (MARC, 1993).

Cragg, Kenneth, *Alive to God: Muslim and Christian Prayer* (Oxford University Press, 1970).

—— *Counsels in Contemporary Islam* (Edinburgh University Press, 1965).

—— *The Pen and the Faith: Eight Modern Muslim Writers and the Qur'an* (George Allen and Unwin, 1985).

Donaldson, Dwight M., *Studies in Muslim Ethics* (SPCK, 1963).

Gladwin, F., *The Gulistan of Saadi*, with an introductory essay by R. W. Emerson (1984).

Guillaume, A., *The Life of the Prophet*, a translation of Ibn Ishaq's *Sirat Rasul Allah* (Oxford University Press, 1970).

—— *The Traditions of Islam* (Universal Books, 1977).

Halm, Heinz, *Shiism* (Edinburgh University Press, 1991).

Iqbal, Muhammad *The Mysteries of Selflessness, A Philosophical Poem*, tr. A. J. Arberry (John Murray, 1953).

Jomier, Jacques, *How to Understand Islam* (SCM Press Ltd., 1989).

Khalid, Fazlun, with O'Brien, Joanne (ed.) *Islam and Ecology* (Cassell, 1992).

Lewis, Philip, *Islamic Britain: Religion, Politics and Identity among British Muslims* (I. B. Tauris, 1994).

Maududi, Abdul A'la, *Towards Understanding Islam* (Islamic Foundation, 1981).

Mernissi, Fatima, *The Forgotten Queens of Islam* (Polity Press, 1993).

—— *The Harem Within: Tales of a Moroccan Girlhood* (Bantam Books, 1995).

—— *Women and Islam: An Historical and Theological Enquiry* (Blackwell, 1991).

Metcalf, B. D., *Islamic Revival in British India, Deoband 1860–1900* (Princeton University Press, 1982).

Mohammad Fadhel Jamali, *Letters on Islam Written by a Father in Prison to his Son* (Oxford University Press; republished 1978).

Musk, Bill, *Passionate Believing: The 'Fundamentalist' Face of Islam* (Monarch Publications, 1992).

—— *The Unseen Face of Islam: Sharing the Gospel with Ordinary Muslims* (MARC, 1989).

Mutahhari, Murtaza Ayatullah, *Fundamentals of Islamic Thought: God, Man and the Universe* (Mizan Press, 1985; Contemporary Islamic Thought, Persian Series).

Niazi, Kausar *Creation of Man* (Sh. Muhammad Ashraf, 1975).

—— *Fundamental Truths* (Sh. Muhammad Ashraf, 1974).

—— *Islam Our Guide* (Sh. Muhammad Ashraf, 1976).

—— *To the Prophet* (Sh. Muhammad Ashraf, 1976).

Nielsen, Jørgen, *Muslims in Western Europe* (Edinburgh University Press, 1992).

Omram, Abdel Rahim, *Family Planning in the Legacy of Islam* (Routledge, 1992).

Padwick, Constance, *Muslim Devotions: A Study of Prayer Manuals in Common Use* (SPCK, 1961).

Parrinder, Geoffrey, *Mysticism in the World's Religions* (Sheldon Press, 1976).

Parshall, Phil, *Inside the Community: Understanding Muslims through Their Traditions* (Baker Books, 1994).

Pickthall, Mohammed, *The Meaning of the Glorious Koran* (Mentor Books, n.d.).

Poston, Larry, *Islamic Da'wah in the West: Muslim Missionary Activity and the Dynamics of Conversion to Islam* (Oxford University Press, 1992).

Qasida Burda (The Prophet's Mantle). Arabic with tr. into various languages, e.g. Urdu, Persian, Turkish, Berber, Swahili, English.

Rahbar, Daud, *God of Justice: Ethical Doctrine in the Qur'an* (Leiden, 1960).

Ritchie, James McL., '*Qasidatu-l-Burda* Translations and Presentation', *Encounter*, nos. 171–2 (Pontificio Istituto di Studi Arabi e d'Islamistica, Rome, Jan./Feb. 1991).

Sheikh, Bilquis, *I Dared to Call Him Father* (Kingsway/STL, 1978).

Shems Friedlander, with al-Hajj Shaikh Muzaffereddin, *Ninety-Nine Names of Allah* (Wildwood House/Graham Brash, 1980).

Smith, Margaret, *Rabi'a the Mystic and her Fellow-Saints* (Cambridge University Press, 1984).

Stacey, Vivienne, *Women in Islam* (Interserve, 1995).

Stoddart, William, *Sufism: The Mystical Doctrines and Methods of Islam* (Thorsons Publishers Ltd., 1976).

Tafti, H. Dehqani, *Design of my World* (United Society for Christian Literature, Lutterworth Press, 1959; 2nd rev. edn., 1982).

Watt, W. Montgomery, *Islamic Philosophy and Theology* (Edinburgh University Press, 1962).

Glossary of Some Key Arabic Words

ahl al-dhimma – protected people; non-Muslims granted special status under Muslim rule

ahl al-kitab – people of the book, that is, Jews and Christians

Al-Mahdi – the 'Guided One'; the rightly guided eschatological figure whose return Muslims expect

Allah – the main Arabic word for God used in the Quran and the Arabic Bible

ayat – sign, verse

bismillah – in the name of God

dar al-harb – the house of war

dar al-Islam – the house of Islam; lands under Muslim rule

dawah – 'invitation' to Islam

dhikr – 'remembrance', the repetition of divine names to foster devotion to Allah

din – the faith of Islam in its religious practices

fatwa – formal legal opinion pronounced by an expert in Islamic law

fiqh – Islamic jurisprudence

hadith – Tradition including what Muhammad said, did or permitted

hadith qudsi – divine tradition ascribed to Allah on Muhammad's authority

hajj – the annual pilgrimage at Mecca in Saudi Arabia, to be performed at least once in a lifetime if economically possible by the Muslim

hazur – chaste

id al-adha – the feast of sacrifice observed seventy days after the end of the fast of Ramadan *id al-fitr* – the feast that is observed at the end of the fast of the month of Ramadan

id al-milad – the feast in celebration of the birth of Muhammad

ijma – consensus or agreement of the Muslim community concerning the interpretation of the application of the teaching of the Quran in a given situation

imam – religious leader

iman – faith in its confession and belief in the heart of the confessor

Isa – the personal name for Jesus in the Quran

Islam – submission (to God). The name of the religion of Muslims

jihad – 'struggle' or 'striving in the way of Allah' by the Muslim against inner evil but more usually against countries or peoples not yet under Islamic rule

jinn – spirit created by God. Some are good but many are evil and greatly feared by Muslims

kalimah – the creed of Islam

karamat – a miracle

khalifah – caliph; the deputy or successor to Muhammad and the leaders of Islam after him. The political leader of Islam

madrasah – mosque school

majlis – open court for meeting a ruler

marabout – a religious leader who exercises miraculous and occult powers. The term is chiefly used in North and West Africa.

masjid – mosque

Muharram – the first month of the Muslim lunar calendar. The death of Husain is commemorated by the Shia Muslims on the tenth day of this month.

mullah – a religious teacher. The term is more commonly used in the Indian subcontinent.

Muslim – a follower of Islam

Quran – the Holy Book of Islam

Ramadan – the ninth month; observed as a month of fasting from daybreak to nightfall when neither food nor drink may be touched except by children under ten, the sick, the very aged, pregnant women and travellers.

salat – the saying of the ordained prayers five times a day at the appointed times *saum* – the act of fasting

shahadah – the 'confession' of the Muslim creed or *kalimah*

shariah – the religious law based on the Quran

shia – 'party'; the Muslim minority which believes that the rightful successor to Muhammad was Ali, the husband of his daughter Fatima

shirk – the greatest of all sins, associating any one or thing with God

sufi – a Muslim mystic

sunnah – habitual practice, norm, usage sanctioned by tradition, setting an example, hence custom

sunni – the largest sect in Islam. Sunnis follow the Quran and the Traditions and are orthodox.

surah – a chapter division of the Quran. There are 114 chapters in the Quran.

talaq – divorce; the pronouncement of the 'divorce' of the woman by the husband

ulama – Muslim theologians; plural of *alim* who is also called mullah, maulvi and maulana

ummah – the single community of Islam; the totality of Muslims

Wahhabi – member of a puritanical reform movement in Islam founded in Arabia

zakat – the legal alms due from every Muslim, generally 2.5 per cent of one's income

Index

Abbasid dynasty 13, 14
Abduh, Muhammad 73
Abdullah Bin Abbas 74
abortion 75
Abu Bakr, Caliph 10, 12, 39
Abyssinia 10, 11
Adab 71
al-Afghani, Jamal al-Din 73, 77
Afghanistan 30–1
Agha Khan 18, 20
Agha Khanis 20
Ahmad, Hazrat Mirza Ghulam 21
Ahmadis 21–2
Ahmed, Professor Akbar S. 104
Alawi Shia 31
Alawis *see* Nusairis
Algeria 33
Ali, Caliph 12
Ali, Maulana Muhammad 79
Allah 4
    attributes 47, 54
    names of 50
    Muslim doctrine 49–51
    revelation in Quran 40
amulets 66
animism 67
apostasy 26–7, 34, 100–1

Arabic language 5, 29, 39
art and architecture 5
al-Ashmawi, Said 99
Assassins *see* Nizaris
astrology 67
ayatollahs 89
Ayyubi dynasty 14
al-Azhar University, Egypt 14, 27, 85
azzan (call to prayer) 56

Baghdad 13
Baha al-Din Naqshbandi 61
Bahais 22–3
Bahrain 11, 27, 28
al-Bajuri 66
Bangladesh 29, 30, 90
    woman prime minister 90
al-Banna, Hasan 97
Bareilly seminary, India 86
Barelwi movement 86
Bhutto, Benazir 30, 84, 90
Bible, and Arabic 9
birth-control 74–6
Bismallah 5, 41, 50
blasphemy 30, 88
Bohras *see* Mustalians
Bourguiba, President 46
Brazil 36
al-Bukhari 44–5, 100

Burnett, David 3–4
Bury seminary 86
Byzantium 11, 12, 13

Cairo, Abbasid caliphate 14
calendar, religious 8, 60–1
caliphate 5, 14
call to prayer (*azzan*) 56
calligraphy 5
celibacy 77
charity *see zakat*
China, North-West 35
Chisti 30
Christianity:
    and environment 74
    missionary mandate, as seen
        by Islam 98–9
    and Muslim Indonesia 33
Christians:
    early, and Muhammad 9
    persecution in Sudan 99
    status in Quran 51, 96
Commonwealth of
        Independent States (CIS)
        32
Communism 30–1, 35
Constantine, Algeria 87
contraception 74–6
conversion to Islam, reasons
        for 96
converts:
    from Islam to Christianity
        33, 99
    to Islam 100
Cragg, Bishop Kenneth 29,
        102–3
cultural centres, Islamic 87

Damascus 13
dawah (mission) 92–3
Deoband seminary, India 85
Deobandis 85, 86

Dervish dances 61
Dervishes *see also* Mawlawis
Dewsbury seminary 86
divorce 78–9
doctrines, fundamental 49–55
Druzes 22
dua (personal prayer) 59–60
dynasties, Islamic 13–14

ecology 73–4
Egypt 27, 91, 99
environment *see* ecology
eschatology 54–5
ethics and morality 69–81
Europe, strategy 94–5
exorcism 84

family planning 74–6
al-Faraj, Abu 74
fast (*sawm*) 58–9
Fatima 12, 13
Fatimid dynasty 13–14, 18
fatwa 88
fiqh (jurisprudence) 78
Five Pillars 56–9
folk Islam 30, 31, 65–8
    Indonesia 33
Forster, E.M. 103
fundamentalists 30, 103
    Turkey 31

al-Ghazali 23–4, 44, 54–5
    on celibacy 77
    ethical teaching 71–2
God:
    Biblical view 47
    Muslim view 49–51
    comparison 50–1
    see also Allah
government, and Islam 91
Gulf Cooperation Council
        (GCC) 27

Gulf States 27–9

Hadith 44–5, 62
  ethics in 70–1
Hafiz al-Asad, President 21
hajj (pilgrimage) 59
al-Halim 66
Hanafi Sunnis 31, 85
Hanifs 10
Hazm, Ibn 90
hereafter 4, 6
Hidden Imam 17
Hijrah (Hegira) 8, 10
  in calendar 60
al-Hilli, Allama 89
Ibn Hisham 45
Holland, Muhtar 96
holy men (*pirs*) 67, 83
Hong Kong 87
human rights 77–9
  and religious toleration
    99–101
humanism *see* secular
  humanism
humanity 51

Ibadis 29
  see also Kharijis
Id al-adha feast 61
Id al-fitr feast 61
ijma (consensus) 78
iman (articles of faith) 54
Imams (religious leaders) 88
India 35
  Sultana 90
Indonesia 32–3, 91
  queens 90
Iqbal, Muhammad 6, 24–5,
    63, 73
Iran 31–2
  abortion in 75
  Shia Muslims 17

Ibn Ishaq 45
Islam:
  centres 26–34
  and Christianity 98–9
  dynasties 13–14
  establishment 8
  minority centres 34–7
  religious branches 15–23
  religious structures 82–91
  spread, factors 96–8
  the word 1
  world-view 1–7
Islamic mission (*dawah*) 92–3
  resources for 95
Islamic Salvation Front 33
Ismailis (Seveners) 17–18
Istanbul 13, 14

Jamaat-i Islami 30, 67, 97–8
al-Jawzi, Ibn 89
Jesus (Isa) 5, 21–2
  mandate 98
  moral teaching not in
    Quran 70
  in Quran 42
  suffering and death 64–5
Jews
  and Muhammad 9, 10–11,
    70
  status in Quran 51, 96
Jiddah, study of families in 28
jihad (holy war) 46, 79–80,
    103
jinn 65, 85
Jinnah, Fatima 77, 90
Jordan and Islam 91

kaaba (Mecca) 11, 57, 59, 67
Kazakhs 35
Kazakhstan 32
Kemal Ataturk 31
Khadija (wife of

Muhammad) 9–10
Kharijis (Ibadis) 15
Khoja Ismailis 19–20
Khomeini, Ayatollah 17, 32, 75, 88
Koran *see* Quran
Korea 93–4
Köse, Ali 95
Kurds 31
Kuwait 27, 28
Kyrgyzstan 32

Lahoris 22
last things 54–5
Liberia 87
Libya 33
Los Angeles mosque 93

madrasahs (mosque schools) 83
Maghrib 33
Mahdi (guided one) 17
Malaysia, book bans 99
Mamluk sultanate 14
marabouts (holy men) 83
marriage 77, 78
Maududi, Abul Ala 90, 98
maulana (scholars) 89
maulvi (scholars) 89
Mawlawis (dancing dervishes) 72
Mecca 8–9, 10, 11, 26
   Kaaba 59
Medina 8, 10, 11, 26
men, roles for 88–9
Mernissi, Fatima 76, 90–1
military action 79–80
Mirzais 22
morality *see* ethics
Morocco 33
mosque schools 83
mosques 5, 57, 82–3, 93

Mount Arafat 59
muezzin 56
Muhammad, Prophet 1–2, 5–6, 8–11
   biographies 45–8
   and ethics 69
   as Ideal Man 70–1
   names for 62
   pattern for traditions 43–4
   reform of Kaaba 67
   revelation of Quran 38
   significance 11
   veneration 62–5
   and women 76
Muhammad ibn Said al-Busiri 63
mujtahids 89
mullahs (scholars) 82–3, 89
al-Munawi, Abd al-Rauf 90
music in Islam 61
Musk, Dr Bill 67
Muslim, meaning of word 1
Muslim Brotherhood (*Al-Ikhwan al-Muslimun*) 67, 97
Muslims:
   and Christians 80
   doctrines 49–55
   numbers 2, 37
Mustalians (Bohras) 20–1
Mutazilites 47
mysticism:
   Islamic 23–4
   of Muhammad 11
   see also Sufism

Naqshbandi 30, 61
Nawaz Sharif 30
Niazi, Maulana Kausar 4, 65–6, 79, 90, 91
Nigeria 34–5
Nimeiri, President 34

Nizam-e-Mustafa 29, 87
Nizaris (Assassins) 19
nur (light) 62–3
Nusairis (Alawis) 21

oil resources 27, 95
Oman 27, 28, 29
Omram, Dr Abdel Rahim 75–6
Organisation of the Islamic
    Conference (OIC) 34
Ottoman Turks 13, 14, 97

Padwick, Constance 47
Pakistan 29–30
    Agha Khanis 20
    Muhammad, veneration 64
    Muhammad Iqbal 24–5
    see also Iqbal, Muhammad
    Nizam-e-Mustafa,
      introduction 87–8
    woman prime minister 90
Parrinder, Geoffrey 11
Pathans 31
Paul, Saint, on Christ 98
People of the Book (*ahl al-
    kitab*) 51, 96
personal prayer (*dua*) 59–60
Philippines 35
Pickthall, M.M. 39–40
pilgrimage (*hajj*) 59
The Pillars of Islam 18
pirs (holy men) 67, 83
politics, women in 90–1
popular Islam *see* folk Islam
population 74–6
possession 84–5
post-modernism, in West 103
prayer, for readers of the
    Quran 47–8
predestination 70
propagation of the Faith 92–
    101

prophethood 4, 5–6
prophets 88

Qadianis 22
Qadiri 30
qasida (poem) 63
Qasim-Shahi line 20
Qatar 27, 28
Quraish tribe 9, 15, 39, 69
Quran 1–2, 38–43
    abrogations 43, 47
    content 42
    on conversion to Islam 100
    on environment 74
    ethical teaching 69–70
    Jesus (Isa) in 42
    law and judgment 43
    on Muhammad 45–6
    prayer for reading 47–8
    questions on 47–8
    recitation 40–1
    revelation 38, 40
    secret doctrines 18
    study 41
    and Sufism 62
    translations 39–40
    on women 76

Rabia al-Adawiya 62, 89
raka (bowing) 57
Ramadan 5, 38, 58–9
    timing 60
Rashid al-Din Sinan 19
rasul (prophet) 88
Raza Khan, Ahmad 86
religious branches of Islam 15–
    23
religious brotherhoods 30
religious leaders:
    female 89–90
    male 88–9
religious police 91

religious structures 82–91
religious toleration 99–101
repentance 53
revelation 65
Ritchie, James 63–4
ritual prayer (*salat*) 56, 57–8
al-Rumi, Jalal al-Din 72
Rushdie, Salman 88, 103–4

Saadi, poem by 102
Saadi, Shaik Muslih al-Din 72
sacred texts 38–48
Saddam Hussein 17, 50

saints 66–7
    female 76–7, 89–90
    shrines 83–4
salat (ritual prayer) 56, 57–8
Salih-al-Din (Saladin) 13, 14, 19, 31
salvation 53–4
Sardar, Ziauddin 80
Satan and jinn 65
Saudi Arabia 4–5, 26–8
    aid to Pakistan 29
    and Islam 91
    mission 95
sawm (fast) 58–9
Scattolin, Giuseppe 89
secular humanism 3, 4, 6–7
    and environment 74
    Maghrib 33
seminaries 85–7
Seoul 93
shahadah (witness) 56–7
shaiks (holy men) 83
Shariah (Islamic law) 4, 5, 87–8
    Nigeria 34–5
    Pakistan 30
    Sudan 34

Sheikh, Bilquis 50
Shia Muslims (Twelvers) 12, 13–14, 17
    Afghanistan 31
    Gulf States 27–8
    Iran 31
    Turkey 30
shirk (idolatry) 52
shrines 83–4
sin, doctrines 52
singleness 77
sira 71
Smith, Dr Margaret 76–7
South America 36
Spain 13
spirituality and worship 56–68
Sudan 33–4
    persecution of Christians 99
Sufis, 23–4, 33, 61–2
    appeal 97
    and ethics 71–2
    favourite verse of Quran 50
    and gender 89
    women saints 77, 89–90
Suleiman the Magnificent 13
Suleyman Chelebi of Bursa 64
Sunnah (text) 43–5, 71
Sunni Moslems 13, 14, 15
    Afghanistan 31
    on God 47
    Gulf State rulers 27, 28
    Sudan 33
    Turkey 30
    former USSR 32

Surhawardi 30
Syria 91
    Ismailis 19, 21

Tablighi Jamaat 86–7
Tajikistan 32
Tajiks 31

texts 38–48
theological colleges 83
Titus, Murray T. 66–7
toleration, Islamic 99–101
Traditions (*hadith*) 43–5
    ethics in 70–1
Tunisia 33, 75
Turkey 31
    and Islam 91
    woman prime minister 90
Turkish Ottoman Empire 13,
    14, 97
Turkmenistan 32

Uighurs 35
ulama (scholars) 89, 90
Umar, Caliph 10, 12, 39
Umayyad dynasty 13
ummah (community) 5
United Arab Emirates 27, 28
United Kingdom, Muslims 36
United Nations Universal
    Declaration of Human
    Rights 78, 99, 101
United States of America 36
unity 4–6
universities and seminaries
    85–7
usury 29, 87
Uthman, Caliph 12, 39
Uzbekistan 32
Uzbeks 31

veiling of women 77
veneration of Muhammad
    62–5

Voice of Islam 95

Wadud (love) 50, 51
Wahhabis 30, 67
al-Walid 11
war 79–80
welfare contribution (*zakat*) 58
witness (*shahadah*) 56–7
women:
    conversion to Islam 95–6
    Iran 32
    in Islam 76–7
    legal rights 87–8
    marriage rights 78
    Muhammad and 11
    Oman 29
    private prayers 57
    roles for 89–91
    saints 76–7
    Saudi Arabia 28
    veiling 77
world-view 3–4
    of Muslims 4–7
worship 56–68

Yemen:
    queens 90
    Zaidis 18

Zafar Ali Khan, Maulana 64
Zaidis 18–19
zakat (welfare contribution) 58
Zayd ibn Thabit 39
Zia ul-Haq, President 29, 87